THE GIRLS' GUIDE TO SEX EDUCATION

The Girls' Guide to
SEX
EDUCATION

Over 100 Honest Answers
to Urgent Questions about Puberty,
Relationships, and Growing Up

Michelle Hope

FOREWORD BY AMY LANG

ILLUSTRATION BY ALYSSA GONZALEZ

ROCKRIDGE
PRESS

CONTENTS

1 Getting to Know You 1

2 What the Heck Is Going on with My Body? 36

3 Girl Stuff 58

4 Healthy Relationships 88

5 Let's Talk about Sex 113

FOREWORD

When I was about eleven, I noticed that my teeny-tiny breasts had lumps! Both of them! The only time I had EVER heard about breast lumps was when someone was talking about breast cancer. I was terrified, and pretty much convinced I had breast cancer.

A bit later, when I was—ahem—"exploring" my vagina, I discovered yet another lump! At the very end of my vagina was this lump that felt like a rubber nose. Once again, I was terrified that something was very wrong with me and my body.

The worst part? I didn't think I had someone I could tell about either of these potentially terminal conditions. My mom wasn't super open about sex, there was no way I'd ask my dad, and my other trusted, knowledgeable adult? She was stressed out by a recent divorce, her own kids, and life in general.

This was in the 80s, and the Internet was not a thing, so I couldn't quickly look up my "symptoms" and get some answers. And because I was so shy and hugely embarrassed, there was *no way* I could get the words out of my mouth and actually ask someone about my worries.

So what *was* up with my boobs and my vagina? My mammary glands were developing along with my other breast tissue, and those were the lumps I felt. And my vaginal rubber-nose-lump? I was touching my cervix.

I was probably close to eighteen or nineteen by the time I learned what my discoveries actually were. There was nothing weird about my boobs, my cervix was where it belonged, and I did not have the world's slowest-growing cancer tumors. But it took far too long after these discoveries to get the answers I needed.

If I had had a book like *The Girls' Guide to Sex Education*, I would have felt so much better about myself and my body. This book—this delightful, helpful, book—answers many questions girls have about their bodies, their developing sexuality, their gender identity, dating, sex, and relationships.

If you are a parent or a trusted, knowledgeable adult and have purchased this gem of a book for a girl in your life— *brava*! It will definitely help you initiate conversations about this subject with your girl. In fact, I would get two copies— one for you and one for her.

You can then memorize and quote Michelle's words about anything covered in this book to your young woman. She won't know you had help (lots of help in some cases), and she will be amazed at your sexuality smarts. Once she hears you say the words, she will learn you are willing and fully capable of talking about sexuality.

You opening your mouth and saying the words is the key to having open sex talks with your girl. Waiting for her to ask questions makes her sexuality education her responsibility; just like you wouldn't let her teach herself how to drive a car without an open conversation about how the car works or the rules of the road, the same goes for sexuality. As you may know for yourself, self-taught sex education is dangerous and potentially disastrous.

If you want your girl to know and understand what healthy sexuality truly is, it's up to you. The information in *The Girls' Guide to Sex Education* will make all the difference for you both.

—AMY LANG, MA
Parenting & Sexuality Educator, founder of Birds & Bees & Kids®

For Parents & Teachers

SEXUALITY. The word alone gives us a range of varying reactions, and when you're young and trying to figure it all out, it can be even more confusing.

Take a moment to think about how sexuality first appeared in your life and who was there to help you understand it all. Was it that awkward gym teacher who used sports euphemisms to explain intercourse? Or perhaps you remember finding porn online. Some of us were lucky enough to have a trusted adult who was open to answering questions about sex, puberty, and all the other tough stuff that comes up in a young person's life. But most of us were left in the dark to figure it out for ourselves.

As a sex educator with a master's degree in human development, and extensive postgraduate training in sexuality, I have spent over ten years writing about sexuality, speaking about sexuality, and developing creative sex-ed programming for youth.

So let me keep it real! I wrote this book for my friends who have children coming of age and hitting puberty. It never ceases to amaze me how often friends hit me up on social media, begging for advice on how to deal with the pesky pubescent problems that come along with having a teenager. While raising a teenager of any gender is a challenge, raising girls comes with added responsibility. Social pressures and media messaging shape their ideals and values in ways that can be detrimental to the development of their self-esteem, body image, and self-respect. It's important for us as parents, loved ones, or stakeholders in a young girl's life to keep in mind that this time of adolescent development can be overwhelming, filled with confusion and lots of questions.

These questions and conversations are hard for young people to bring up with adults. And it can be uncomfortable for parents, mentors, teachers, and stakeholders to initiate discussions about these matters. It's nerve-racking, even scary. We might fear we won't have all the answers to a young girl's questions about sexuality. We might feel emotionally overwhelmed if we don't want to think about her becoming sexually active too soon.

I've found it's best to remain open and nonjudgmental and to fight the urge to jump to conclusions. More often than not, young people are seeking information on something they've heard from peers. It's okay if you don't have all the answers; in fact, not having all the answers can be an opportunity for you and your young person to seek out those answers together.

I advise you, as a parent or teacher, to read as much of this book as possible, especially the chapter about sex, in order to be able to engage in conversations about the questions provided at the end of each chapter. These questions are designed to allow readers to think critically about the decisions they make concerning their health, the relationships they build, and their values.

When a young person identifies us as the adult they want to talk to about their questions, it means they trust us. It's our responsibility to show up for them. It might not seem like it, but I can assure you that those young people do *want* to have conversations with you. According to the most recent study,[1] 52 percent of children ages 12 to 15 said their parents have the most influence on their thoughts when it comes to sex, with friends far behind at 17 percent. Interestingly, the study highlighted that for the subsequent age group of 16 to 18, parental influence drops to only 32 percent. That's why, as parents and stakeholders, we must capitalize on the time and influence we have sooner rather than later.

Let me be clear: The process of puberty will not be easy on you, and it will be even more difficult for your young person. So before we go any further, I'll give you a few recommendations that are essential to keep in mind.

First, *do not* overreact. It might be difficult, but do your best to remember that overreacting will only exacerbate the issue. Of course young people do stupid things (just like you did in your youth!), but they need you to support them, especially through their mistakes. Judgment does no good in most if not all situations, so no judgment is the way to go.

It's also important to listen. I mean really listen, not just with your ears but also with a loving heart and a patient mind. This type of listening requires that you put your phone down, turn off the TV, and tune in to this amazing young person who is developing into an adult in front of you. If you're not careful, you'll blink your eyes and your young person will be an adult, out of your home and out of your hands.

I developed this book using three basic principles:

1. Sexuality is not a dirty word

Sexuality is an organic part of what makes us human. It is a complex thing, with multiple factors that impact a person's development. We must start with the understanding that sexuality touches not only the biological but also the psychological, sociological, emotional, and even spiritual variables of life. There is no "right time" to start conversations about sexuality; they should be frequent and ongoing. From the womb to the tomb, sexuality is a part of our daily lives.

2. National Sexuality Education Standards

My decision to include specific information in this book was guided by the National Sexuality Education Standards developed by the organization Future of Sex Ed.[2] The standards comprise seven key topics: Anatomy and Physiology, Puberty and Adolescent Development, Identity, Pregnancy and Reproduction, Sexually Transmitted Diseases and HIV, Healthy Relationships, and Personal Safety.

3. Reproductive-justice framework

Reproductive justice, according to the authors of the *Reproductive Justice Briefing Book*,[3] is the complete physical, mental, spiritual, political, social, and economic well-being of women and girls, based on the full achievement and protection of women's human rights.

After reading the above information, you might be thinking, *Aren't our kids too young to be having these conversations?* I can tell you that it's never too soon to talk with them about our belief in their abilities and the values we hold for relationships. It is also never too soon to provide them with medically accurate information about their bodies and development.

Creating a safe space for a young person to ask questions and explore their own thoughts with an adult can lead to healthier social and emotional outcomes as they move through adolescence. This book provides timely, age-appropriate, and medically accurate information. It contains real questions that teens are asking about sex and sexuality, some taken directly from the students I've worked with over the years, others asked often by youth online.

There's no right time to begin these awkward and sometimes challenging conversations, and this book is a resource to ease some of the discomfort that might be felt by both you and your young person. We live in a time in which we're bombarded by all kinds of messages about sex and sexuality. When you encounter those messages, use them as an opportunity to let your young person know you believe in their ability and remind them of what healthy relationships look like.

INTRODUCTION

So it begins. Puberty is the beginning of the journey to the rest of your life. Will it be easy? In all likelihood, no. I totally get that some of the things you're about to go through are going to suck. It's not always easy to move through life with a positive self-image and a belief in yourself.

That being said, I want to help make your life easier. I hope you will use this book as a reference as you move from puberty into adolescence and high school, maybe even college.

I completely understand that at times the subject matter in this book might make you feel weird, upset, angry, or just downright frustrated. That's totally normal. A lot of the things we're going to talk about in this book will be really raw, and I'm not going to sugarcoat anything.

I also want to remind you that, although it might be difficult or awkward, your parents or other loved ones who got you this book are willing and ready to have those tough conversations. You should never be afraid to talk to your family or other trusted adults in your life because all adults have gone through this turbulent time you're about to enter. In fact, I designed this book to give you opportunities to have conversations with your Trusted, Knowledgeable Adult(s), or as I like to say, your TKA. That's anybody in your life who you feel is trustworthy—someone you can count on, someone who wants the best for you and won't put you in harm's way. Most importantly, your trusted, knowledgeable adult should believe in you and your abilities.

I'm passionate about this book because I believe it will be a great instruction manual to help you through what will probably be one of the most challenging times of your life. I'm talking about middle school and, let's face it, probably high school as well. This book should be used as a resource anytime you or your friends have any questions, especially about sex, relationships, or puberty. Whatever your questions are, I've done my best to provide a really practical answer. If you want to read the book cover to cover, feel free, but I suggest looking through it first and flipping to the questions that you really need to have answered right then and there.

I also recommend journaling or writing down how you feel about this new information. Journaling is a great way for you to work through some of the challenges that may come up as you start to go through puberty. At the end of each chapter, there are five open-ended questions for you to think about. I recommend discussing them with a TKA—someone close to you, someone you trust, someone who wants the best for you. I want you to feel confident that you have the correct answers to all your questions about sex.

It's my hope that by reading this book, you will learn that it's totally okay to march to the beat of your own drum and that you are the star of your life—so let's start living it!

chapter 1

Getting to Know You

I understand what you're going through. Entering puberty was one of the most difficult times of my life. I felt like a total fish out of water, flailing around and gasping for air. This chapter is about knowing yourself for who you are and embracing change as a natural part of life, so you don't have to do as much flailing as I did.

Am I normal?

The very definition of normal is "conforming to social norms," which is a fancy way of saying "doing things that a lot of other people do." But one of the coolest things about living in our society is that the new normal is to be different. There are so many ways to embrace the things that make you unique and stand out from the pack. I encourage you not to wonder if you're normal or ordinary. Instead, look at how you're extraordinary. Of course, for now it might seem like there's only one way to be normal, and that's to act like all the people around you. But the world is a big place, and what's normal where you live might not be considered normal just a few towns away. As you grow up, you'll come to realize that you and only you are in control of your life, and that you have the ability to decide what's right and "normal" for you.

Will I ever feel like I belong?

As humans, we all want to belong. It's a totally natural feeling to have. As you get older, you'll probably find there are times when you feel like you really belong to one group and then maybe as time goes on, you grow out of that group and find another. I think the desire to belong is really about being comfortable with yourself, getting along with the people you hang out with, and finding groups that appreciate all your gifts and talents. That's how you can feel like you belong. If you're struggling to find a sense of belonging, you can go out and find groups of friends by joining clubs, playing school sports, or getting involved with community service. Oftentimes, there are people out there just waiting for someone as unique as you to be a part of their group.

Am I good enough?

We're all born "good enough." If you're worried you're not good enough at a specific task, like playing soccer or learning geometry, it's important to remember that it's very rare to be good at something on the first try. If you don't give up and you continue to practice and try, then you're always good enough. Even if you're terrible at it, you're still good enough because you made a choice to not give up.

Who am I?

Understanding who you are is like life—it's not a race, it's a journey, and on that journey, you'll have ups and downs, happy times, sad times, and really crappy times. But it's how you pick yourself back up that will shape who you are as a person. Even as an adult, I ask myself on a daily basis, "Who am I?" When you consider how often television and media tell us who we should be, it's no surprise that sometimes we can get a little confused about it, even as adults. One great way to tap back into who you are is to journal. Identify what makes you feel happiest and brings you joy, and remember: You don't have to know who you are today or tomorrow. Who you are will change as you age, and you have the rest of your life to figure it out. Ten years from now, you're not going to be the same person you are today. That's how it's supposed to be. That's kind of the beauty of getting older! You can always redefine yourself.

Why do I feel like everything is changing?

Everything *is* changing, and it's a marvelous, challenging journey toward your adult life. Your brain and body are changing and growing faster than at almost any other time in your life, second only to when you were a baby. The very way you look at the world is changing. Yes, it's awkward, but you can lean into the awkwardness and discover who you are right now and who you might become as an adult. Of course, this can be a very scary time. That's why it's important to stay informed and have an adult or mentor to go talk to. The next few years will be kind of like a roller coaster with ups and downs, but hold on. Don't be afraid to ask for support from the people around you, and try to enjoy the experiences that come with puberty and adolescence. Those experiences will play a large role in how you develop into an adult.

Why am I starting not to like my oldest friends?

As we grow up, our likes and dislikes change—and they should! The more we learn new things and expand our experiences, the more we might find ourselves evolving and changing. That means our interests might vary, and sometimes the people around us might not be moving in the same direction as we are. It's totally normal to grow out of your friends, like you did last year's sweater. It doesn't mean you don't like them anymore. It just means that you like doing different things than they do, and perhaps that will change the dynamic of how much you hang out with them. If your friends are not supportive of your goals, if they treat you poorly or talk about you behind your back, then they're not your true friends. But the end of a friendship doesn't have to be a burning flame of drama. Sometimes friendships just end because you're growing one way and your friend is growing another way.

What do I do if people are talking about me behind my back?

This is a problem even adults struggle with sometimes. It always feels bad when someone talks about you behind your back, especially if they're saying things that aren't true. Let's face it: If someone is talking about you behind your back, that's the first indicator that they're not really your friend. As we grow up and experience others talking about us in one way or another, we learn that most times, the chatter will die down as long as we don't react. It's important to remember that you cannot control what other people do. You can only control how you react—and make sure you don't talk about others behind their backs.

However, if you feel threatened by people talking about you, or if the rumors become overly aggressive, you may be experiencing bullying. It really doesn't matter if it takes place at school, online, or at work. Bullying is a form of harassment, and you should tell your trusted, knowledgeable adult about it. No one should have to experience bullying or harassment, and there are laws to protect you.

What makes someone a girl?

Most people born with a vagina, uterus, and all the other body parts we'll be talking about in this book are girls. And most people born with a penis and other male reproductive organs are boys. If that's true for you, then you're cisgender, or cis. But sometimes people can be born with a vagina and feel like they're actually a boy, or be born with a penis and feel like they're actually a girl. If that's true for you, then you're transgender, or trans. Throughout this book, we'll be talking about things that happen to a girl's body as she grows up. These things might not all be true for trans girls, though many trans girls and women will take hormones like estrogen and progesterone, so they can go through some of the same changes cis girls naturally go through during puberty, like growing breasts. Whether you're cis or trans, you're awesome the way you are.

Is it okay if I don't like girly stuff?

One of the things that makes you *you* is that you like what you like. Don't ever feel that just because you're a girl, you can't like sports or you have to like fashion. Some people like football and BMX, some like doing makeup and playing dress-up, and a lot of people like all those things at once. They're not "boy" and "girl" things, they're human things. It's important not to believe the hype when society and the media try to tell you what you should like. Anyone of any gender can like what they like.

Am I pretty?

You are the most beautiful you that there is in the world. Don't believe anyone who tells you differently. Magazines, television, and social media try to tell us what is beautiful and how we should identify beauty, when really, you define beauty. It's important to identify what you like about yourself, starting with the inside stuff—your personality, your kindness, your smarts. Identify what you think is beautiful about your body. Every body is different, and you should love all parts of your body. Stretch marks, big boobs, little boobs—it's all beautiful because it's yours. Not to mention you're not going to look like this forever. If you're somebody who's struggling to accept your body—in my case, it was my hair—one day you'll figure it out and it'll be okay. In any case, looks often fade. It's what's inside that counts. What makes you beautiful is your integrity, your honesty, your generosity, and your kindness. Those are beautiful characteristics that no one can ever take from you and that will never go out of style.

Why do I always think I look so fat?

Our society gives us a lot of very unhealthy ideas about what our bodies should look like, but you can't compare yourself to what you see on TV, movies, ads, or other media. We're all born with various unique body types that we get due to our genetic makeup (the specific set of characteristics we inherit from our parents), and we usually don't have much control over them. Seeing as how you're approaching or beginning puberty, you should know that women's bodies tend to carry a little more fat than male bodies, especially around the hips, waist, buttocks, and breasts. That's because we need the fat in case we ever want to have a baby. You might notice you're beginning to get a little cellulite around those areas too. That's totally normal—in fact, cellulite is a genetic thing, and even skinny people get it. And as you start your menstrual cycle, there might be certain days of the month when you feel more bloated and uncomfortable than usual. That's totally normal too. When it comes to weight, what's important is being healthy and loving yourself, not whether you think you look fat.

What if I don't like my body or the way I feel?

Not liking your body while going through puberty is like not looking forward to going to the dentist—we've all had that feeling once or twice in our lives. As you develop and go through puberty, there are times when you will feel bloated, gassy, achy, or just plain uncomfortable. New hormones may make you feel strange new feelings you've never felt before. You might feel like you don't recognize parts of your own body, or that your body has turned against you. This is an amazing, miraculous part of becoming a woman. It also totally sucks. Getting enough sleep, exercising, and eating a well-balanced diet can help improve your mood. As for your hormones, as you continue to get your period more regularly, they'll eventually start to regulate, and you'll get a little more familiar with some of those feelings.

Why do I feel sad/angry?

Your body, brain, and emotions are basically having a dance battle right now, and that dance battle will continue through puberty and probably through most of high school. It's completely normal to feel angry and sad sometimes, but it's how we communicate those feelings to other people that matters. You're entering a time in your life where you're starting to have more and more of your own thoughts and opinions, separate from those of your parents and other loving adults in your life. When you feel like the adults in your life don't understand you, you have to check in on how you're communicating your thoughts and if you're using too much emotion. Anger and sadness are emotions that can inhibit us from clearly communicating our needs and wants to the people around us, so we have to be mindful of how we express both of those emotions.

Why do I feel like I'm not in control of my emotions?

You probably feel like you're not in control of your emotions because as you grow up and enter middle school, and then high school, you're actually not really in control of your emotions! Your body, brain, and hormones are changing a lot as they work together to get you ready for the rest of your life. It's kind of like driving a car with a blindfold on— you really don't have any idea where you're going or if you'll hit a roadblock that triggers an emotional overload. The best thing for you to do is acknowledge when you feel emotionally out of control, and maybe even write down some notes about it. Being able to identify what really sets your emotions off can help you plan for best responses, so your emotions won't consume you and cloud your judgment or decision-making ability.

You can also work on the practice of meditation, which is when you stop and take a moment to clear the mind. Taking a pause or removing yourself from a situation to clear your thoughts can really save you from an emotional meltdown. To deepen this skill, you must practice, just like you would with a sport or any other skill. Before bed, turn off your phone and play some relaxing music (best if it's without words), and just let your mind clear. It won't be easy when you start, but it's totally worth it. It takes everyone, even adults, a long time to master their emotions, but it's a skill that will serve you for the rest of your life.

How can I feel better about myself?

There's no quick solution to feeling better about yourself. Rather, it's work that continues throughout middle school, high school, and probably your adult life as well. However, there are some things you can do to help pump up your mood. For starters, your brain and body are going through a lot right now, so you need to be sure you're getting enough sleep, eating a balanced diet—yes, that means fruits and vegetables—and drinking plenty of water. Exercise also releases chemicals called endorphins in your brain, which make you feel happier. When I feel down or sad, I like to go on a bike ride or hang out with friends. It's important to surround yourself with people who love and care about you, people who see the greatness in you and can remind you of how awesome it is to be alive. Feeling bad about yourself is a normal experience. You just have to remember that feeling down is an emotion, like any other, and emotions are momentary, not permanent.

How do I know if I'm struggling with a mental-health issue?

Mental-health issues can be tricky. That's why people who work in the mental-health profession go to school for many years. The first step to identifying a mental-health issue is recognizing that something doesn't feel right. Maybe you feel sad more often than you used to, or maybe you feel like you'll never be happy again. The second step is talking to someone about it—your parents, your teachers, your guidance counselor, or another trusted, knowledgeable adult. The adults in your life are there to help you get the resources you need to be your best self. Don't be afraid to ask for help with this issue. Taking care of your mental health is so important for you to live a happy, healthy life. Seeking help from professionals doesn't mean you are "crazy." What's really nonsensical is knowing there's a problem but not getting help. Going through puberty, middle school, and high school can make anyone very confused—it's totally normal to feel out of sorts during this time! It's important to have someone you can talk to, and they can help you decide if you need professional help.

Why do I sometimes feel like I want to die?

There is nothing that is so bad that you should want to take your life. Yes, everybody has embarrassing moments they wish would disappear or days where they feel really, really down, and that's entirely normal. But feelings about wanting to die are not feelings I want to identify as normal, especially if those feelings last or linger. If you have those feelings, it's very important that you talk to somebody about them, and I don't just mean a friend—I mean a parent, teacher, guidance counselor, or mental-health professional. Middle school and high school can be tough. You're going to have down days sometimes. In fact, you're going to have down days from time to time for the rest of your life. But you don't want to stay down, so if you're having these feelings, talk to somebody. If nobody is available and you need to talk to somebody right away, you can always call the National Suicide Prevention Lifeline 24/7 for free and confidential support from a trained professional at 1-800-273-8255.

Does the amount of likes and followers I have on social media really matter?

Followers and likes on social media can be fun, but they don't compare to the really important things like loving yourself and understanding that you have family and friends around you who love you. What matters in real life—and online life, for that matter—is not followers, ratings, or likes. It's surrounding yourself with people who believe in you, support you, and make you feel good when they're around.

Do I have to post online to be cool?

Posting your life online doesn't make you cool. In fact, trying to post the cool moments of your life might distract you from actually enjoying those moments. I once got the opportunity to meet our president, and I almost missed it because I was too busy trying to make sure I captured a picture of our handshake on my phone. We don't live our lives to post online—we live our lives to experience life. Of course, it can be nice to have pictures of great times, but it's better to have a great time than stress out about what you're going to post.

Is it wrong to compare myself to others?

I know it can sometimes be hard not to compare yourself to others when you're scrolling through Instagram or other social-media apps. In the wild world of the web, people often just post the highlights of their lives. They don't show you the real, wrong, or gritty parts of what it took to get them to the good times. There are also quite a few ways to manipulate the reality of the situation on TV, in pictures, and through social media, so it doesn't make sense to compare your life to someone else's when you don't even know what their life is truly like. In the end, comparing yourself to others only distracts you from your dreams and goals. You have to remember that as long as you are dedicated and determined, you can achieve whatever you want. It's possible—but it won't look picture perfect. When you find that you're starting to compare yourself to someone else, I want you to dig deep and think about all the things that make you unique. Focus on those characteristics, and remember that they are uniquely yours.

How do I know if I'm gay?

If you find yourself wanting to date, kiss, and maybe some-day get married to a girl, congratulations, you might be gay! You might also be bisexual, meaning you're interested in dating both guys and girls. Whether you're straight, gay, or somewhere in between, you're perfect the way you are. Understanding sexual orientation and feelings of love takes years, so don't feel rushed. If you find yourself attracted to the same sex, that's perfectly normal and okay. You're in a very exploratory time of your life, and you don't have to make a decision on whom you want to date today, tomorrow, or ever, really. What's important is that you remember to love yourself and spend time with people who love and respect you for who you are, no matter whom you love.

How do I tell my parents I'm gay?

Coming out as gay can be difficult, no matter how old you are. In fact, I have adult friends who still haven't told their parents they're gay. So if you're ready to come out to your parents, I want to applaud you for being bold and knowing yourself well. If you don't think your parents are going to react kindly, I suggest finding a trusted adult ally who can help you talk about your feelings and practice how you're going to tell your parents. I hope your parents understand that you're perfect the way you are, no matter whom you love. But the hard truth is that sometimes parents aren't willing to accept their kids' sexual orientation. If it doesn't feel safe to tell your parents, it's my hope that you can turn to another trusted, knowledgeable adult in your life as an ally and support system for you, in terms of your sexual orientation and beyond.

Is it okay to have a crush on my coach or teacher?

Having a crush on a coach, teacher, or other adult that you work with in your life is completely normal. You might have feelings for these people because they care for you, they respect you, and they believe in you—but that doesn't mean that they're romantically or sexually attracted to you. In fact, if a teacher or coach expresses his or her sexual feelings toward you, it means that person is not someone you can trust or someone you should spend time around. Talk to a trusted, knowledgeable adult about it right away.

Am I a "slut" if I've already had sex or done other stuff?

As teenagers get older, it's normal to start trying out sexual stuff. No matter if you've already had sex or done other stuff in any context, you should never feel like a "slut." Perhaps you rushed into something physical. You need not worry. It's happened to the best of us—even as adults, we sometimes get caught up in the moment. It absolutely doesn't mean you're bad or dirty.

However, you should never do anything you don't want to. You always have the right to say no. It doesn't matter if you've already had sex with a person or not. If you don't feel good about what's going on, you can always take a break, step back, and choose abstinence for as long as you want. If people around you are saying or doing things that make you feel like you can't say no, you should avoid those people, tell them to stop, and not hesitate to talk to a TKA.

Who can I trust when I have a problem?

You're about to go on an incredible journey called adolescence, and it's time for you to start identifying the allies in your life. You have to start by knowing that you can always go to your parents when you have a problem. Of course, they might not always be the happiest when you tell them what your problem is, but they will always love you and be there for you. If you don't feel like you can go to your parents, I recommend that you find another trusted, knowledgeable adult (TKA) in your life to talk to—a family member, teacher, guidance counselor, coach, or any adult who believes in you and wants the best for you. A TKA would never ask you to do something that could get you in trouble with your parents, with the police, or with your school. They will also never ask you to do anything sexually or physically that will make you feel uncomfortable. People you can identify as TKAs are people who are actively helping you achieve your goals, believe in you, and want the best for you.

Can I really talk to my parents about sex?

Yes, you can really talk to your parents about sex. In fact, you *should* talk to your parents about sex. It might not be an easy conversation, and it's most definitely going to be an awkward conversation, but your parents are there to help you get the resources you need. However, I do recommend that you prepare. You can do this by writing down any questions you might have and practicing what you're going to say. If you want to, you can use this book to help explain your questions. Sometimes it's best to prepare your parents for the conversation before you have it. You could send them a text with a link to an article you found online and say, "I have some questions about this. Can we chat?" If you feel weird about your parents knowing a sex-related question is coming directly from you, another great way to start the conversation is to say, "My friend at school told me . . ." and then insert any topic that you have a question about. That can help you and your parents feel more comfortable discussing a tricky topic head-on.

How do I get my parents to stop treating me like a baby?

This time of your life is filled with a lot of changes in your body, in your mind, and in your emotions. Of course you might be freaking out. But let me tell you: Your parents are freaking out too! It's hard for them to let go of the idea that you're their little baby girl. They'll say things like, "I remember just yesterday I was changing her diaper." As they help you through this time, you can help them too. The best way to get your parents to not treat you like a baby is to communicate in the most mature way possible. Listening and speaking to your parents respectfully is a pretty good indicator that you're in control of your emotions. Taking on extra chores around the house and completing tasks in a timely fashion proves to your parents that you're mature enough to accept additional responsibilities and freedoms outside of the house.

What is high school like?

For some people, high school is the highlight of their lives. For others, like myself, high school is not so fun. Sometimes it's even terrible. I was kind of an awkward kid, and I didn't really fit in with many people. But I did involve myself in a lot of extracurricular activities, clubs, and sports to help distract myself from how much I hated high school. Maybe, like me, you'll have more fun the more active you are. Maybe you'll be more focused on schoolwork or an after-school job. Either way, I learned a lot, and I lived to tell about it, and you will too.

Is this ever going to get any easier?

Life always flows, kind of like the high tide and low tide of the ocean. Some days will be easier than others, and some days will be harder, but as long as you can remember who you are and surround yourself with a solid support system, you'll be able to get through the tough times. Don't ever be afraid to ask your trusted, knowledgeable adult or other individuals to help you out.

Do I have to get married someday?

You have all the time in the world to decide whether or not you want to get married and who you might want to get married to. It's important to remember that marriage is a legally binding contract that comes with a lot of adult responsibilities, not just emotionally, physically, and mentally, but also financially. Marriage is a lot more work than you might think. People who are married have problems and often struggle, but marriage signifies their commitment to make it work.

Before jumping into any relationship, be sure you're in love with yourself. Being in a romantic relationship with another person won't mean you feel great about yourself all of a sudden. Likewise, being single doesn't mean you're not a whole person. You don't ever have to get married if it's not what you want.

How do I achieve my dreams?

Achieving dreams is not as easy as it might seem. Television, Instagram, and Facebook can make us believe that all the celebrities and influential people we look up to hit it big overnight. News flash: They didn't. Oftentimes, the public doesn't see the stories of the trials and failures of the people we respect the most because nobody wants to talk about the work it takes to achieve your goals. Dreams are just goals without plans. So the first step to achieving your goals is to make a plan. Identify other people who are successful at what you want to do, and then study their careers. When you're willing to dedicate your time, and make sacrifices if necessary, anything is possible.

♥ When you were my age did you ever feel like no one heard you or understood you?

♥ What do you find most unique about me?

♥ What can I do to build your trust in me?

chapter **2**

What the Heck Is Going on with My Body?

Puberty is the time in your life when your body goes through some pretty extreme changes as your brain, body, and emotions develop into maturity. Let me warn you: There are going to be moments when it sucks bad—real bad! But if you just hold on, there's so much to look forward to—like your whole adult life! In this chapter, we'll talk about some of the ways your body changes during this part of your life.

What is puberty?

Puberty is the time in life when people become sexually mature, which means their bodies become able to make a baby. This process takes a few years, and it usually happens between the ages of 10 and 14. It involves big physical, mental, and emotional changes. For girls, those changes include developing breasts and starting to have periods.

When does puberty start?

Puberty starts at varying times for all people. On average, puberty for girls takes place between the ages of 10 and 14 or so, but don't worry if you fall outside this age range. How puberty looks is something that will vary from girl to girl, and no one experiences it in the same way. You might start to notice you're developing breasts, growing hair in your armpits or vagina area, and producing stronger body odor than before. If you haven't already, you'll soon get your period, which is when you bleed from your vagina for several days every month.

Why is my body changing?

Your body is changing because you have begun the process of becoming an adult woman. As a young girl entering puberty, your body—specifically, your ovaries (where you produce the egg cells that could potentially develop into babies)—begin to produce more hormones called estrogen and progesterone. A hormone is a special type of chemical in your body that's super important to your reproductive system. Estrogen and progesterone are the building blocks of becoming an adult woman who can one day have a child of her own, if she wants to.

Why do I want to sleep all the time?

During puberty, you need a lot of sleep because your body is changing and developing so quickly. Puberty throws off your circadian rhythm, which is the system in your body that tells your brain when it's time to sleep and when it's time to wake up. Although it's probably harder to get up in the morning for you right now, there are some things you can do to help yourself get a good night's sleep. The bright light from screens can trick your circadian rhythm into thinking it's daytime and prevent you from getting sleepy, so it's important to stop using your tablet, computer, or cell phone before bedtime. It's also a good idea to turn your phone off prior to going to sleep, so you aren't tempted to start texting or scrolling through Instagram instead of getting the rest your body needs. Reading a book can help too, but remember, it has to be a printed book, not one you're reading on a screen.

Why am I growing (or not growing) in height?

Puberty is typically the time in your life when you grow to your full adult height. But everyone grows at different rates. You might have a huge growth spurt one year, or you might just keep growing a little taller every year. Your height is decided mostly by your genetics, which means you can't really do anything to make yourself taller or shorter. Remember, all bodies are different, and yours is great no matter what height it is.

Why do my stretch marks itch?

Ah, good old stretch marks. We all have them, and they're totally normal. They're caused by rapidly gaining or losing weight, or, for teens going though puberty, they can also be associated with sudden growth spurts. The itching is usually caused by dry skin. To prevent that, after you shower, pat excess water off your skin and apply moisturizer. Keeping your skin hydrated will help with the itching and visibility of the stretch marks.

When should I start shaving?

There's no "right" time to start shaving—heck, you don't ever have to shave at all if you don't want to! But during puberty, you'll notice that you're starting to grow thicker hair on your legs, armpits, crotch, and maybe other places like your upper lip. Many women choose to shave or wax some or all of that hair off, while others don't.

How do I shave?

Let me be real about this hair thing. Shaving and other forms of hair removal are personal preference. Having hair everywhere is fine, and I don't want you to feel pressured to remove it. Sometimes I shave, but sometimes I don't, and it doesn't make me feel any less pretty. But shaving is a common part of adulthood for men and women, so let's talk about it! Whether you're shaving your armpits, legs, or anywhere else, you'll probably nick yourself a few times, meaning that you'll get a small cut from the razor. These cuts tend to bleed a lot, but don't worry, they're not serious. I would suggest using an electric razor at first until you get the hang of it. It may not remove as much hair as you want, but it's safer.

When it comes to pubic hair, some women remove all their pubic hair, some remove just the hair that would be visible when wearing a swimsuit, and some remove no hair. Your pubic hair does have a biological purpose—it protects your vagina against bacteria—but if you choose to remove it, that's okay too. Pubic hair tends to be much coarser and curlier than the hair on your head, which means that when you shave it, there's a high chance of getting ingrown hairs, razor burns, or razor bumps, all of which are pretty unpleasant. There are also other ways to remove hair, like waxing and hair-removal creams. When it comes to shaving, you should probably talk to your trusted, knowledgeable adult to ask what their recommendation might be.

Why is there new hair growing under my armpits and between my legs? Is that normal?

Hair is a natural part of being human. In fact, did you know that when babies are developing in the womb, they're covered in hair called "lanugo," which they usually shed before they're born? As we grow older, we have a few different kinds of hair on our bodies, like head hair, eyebrow hair, and the short, fine "peach fuzz" you find all over your body. Around puberty, you also start growing hair in your vagina area, which is called "pubic hair," as well as in your armpits, which most people just call "armpit hair." Some girls shave their leg hair and armpit hair—and some don't. It can be surprising to have this brand-new feature on your body, but however much or little pubic or armpit hair you have, it's completely normal.

How can I get rid of my acne?

Acne can be caused by many different factors. It could be that your skin is producing too much oil because your hormones are changing so fast as you move through puberty. Dead skin cells could be clogging your pores. Or it could be something else entirely. The key to maintaining healthy skin is to maintain a healthy body, and that comes from the inside out. Drinking plenty of water, eating a well-balanced diet, and washing your face twice a day should help to some extent. If you still have bad acne, don't hesitate to ask a doctor about it. But most people going through adolescence do have some acne no matter what, and it usually goes away when you're an adult.

Would exercise help?

Exercise helps everything! During exercise, your brain releases a lot of different chemicals that fight stress, boost energy, and even improve your mood. That's why after we exercise we often feel upbeat, at ease, and clearheaded. While puberty can be pretty stressful, with hormones causing a lot of mood swings, exercising can help make you less stressed and moody, so be sure to stay active. You can do this by joining a sport at school, signing up for a dance class, or just taking a walk with friends or family. If you're not into group stuff, I recommend doing some stretching every morning before school and once again before bed. I personally like to turn on my favorite music and dance in my room like no one is watching—well, no one *is* watching, and I have no sense of rhythm, so that's probably for the best. But when I'm done working up a good sweat, I'm always in a better mood.

Should I use all the products people tell me to use?

No! Use products that are good for you. When it comes to products, it's going to be a bit of a trial-and-error process, but never be afraid to ask your trusted, knowledgeable adult for advice or help. If you're lucky enough to have a woman as your TKA, there's a high likelihood she's gone through her own trial and error with various women's products, from shampoo to tampons, and so much more. What's most important to remember is that companies and advertisements will try to tell you you're not good enough and that you need to buy their products so you can be better, but they're wrong. Remember, your body is yours, and it's great. You don't need a certain kind of shampoo or mascara to make you beautiful.

Why do we grow boobs?

As you hit puberty, your body starts changing in response to the hormones estrogen and progesterone. This includes your boobs. Remember, puberty is the time when your body becomes able to make a baby, and breasts are a part of that. (They let us produce milk to feed babies, after all.) Sometimes, while your breasts are developing and sometimes before or during your periods, you'll experience discomfort, a feeling of heaviness, or even pain. Don't worry, it's all totally normal.

Why do my friends have breasts and not me?

Breasts develop at different times and rates—even in the same body! As you go through puberty, don't be shocked if one breast is bigger than the other. It's completely normal to have them grow at different rates for a while. Boobs come in all shapes, sizes, and even densities, and that's all perfectly fine. It's my hope that you love your lady lumps no matter how big or small they are.

How do you know when your period is going to start?

Your period is when you bleed from your vagina for several days every month, and don't worry, we'll talk about it in more detail in the next chapter. The tricky thing about periods is you never really know when the first one is going to start, but if you've started to grow breasts and pubic hair, your period will probably come soon. The average age of a girl's first period is about twelve, but that's just an average. Some girls might start as young as age eight or even six, while other girls might not start their period until age sixteen. There's no magic number or way to predict the exact day you will step into womanhood with your first menstrual cycle (period). I suggest you ask your mom or another trusted, knowledge-able adult about when they started their period, as I'm sure they can tell you how it just popped up on them out of the blue as well.

Do boys get a period like me?

No, boys do not get a period, because you get your period when your uterus sheds its lining, and they don't have a uterus like girls do. We'll talk more about it in chapter 3.

What happens to boys during puberty?

It's normal for you to wonder what happens to boys during puberty. Just to reassure you, boys are going though a roller coaster of changes, just like you are. However, the process happens slightly later for boys than girls. Obviously, because girls and boys have different body parts, there are different physical changes. But some of the changes are the same. Like girls, during the onset of puberty boys will experience drastic changes in height and weight, and both boys and girls experience new hair growth under their arms and around their genitals.

There will also be changes in the brain and the production of hormones, although boys experience an increase in the hormone testosterone instead of estrogen. Testosterone helps boys develop in areas such as sperm production, muscle mass, growth of girth (thickness) and length of penis, testicular (balls) growth, facial hair, and the deepening of their voices. Yet boys will go through emotional and mental changes in a very similar way to girls.

If you want a full rundown of the differences in girls and boys, talk to a trusted, knowledgeable adult. There is a lot of information that you can find online, but it's best if you do Internet searches with an adult who can help you find reliable sites, as there are some sites out there that could provide incorrect information.

Why does it feel like I have a stomach virus when I have my period?

Well, there's a complicated scientific explanation involving hormones, but here's what you really need to know: Before and during a menstrual cycle, a lot of women may experience gas, diarrhea, stomach cramping, or constipation. All women are different, and we all experience different things during our period, but digestive issues are an entirely normal part of the process.

♥ When you were my age did you
ever feel like your body was
developing differently from
your friends' bodies?

♥ What's one thing you wish someone
would have told you about going
through puberty?

♥ What is the best way to express
that I need some privacy?

chapter 3

Girl Stuff

In chapter 2, we talked about some changes your body goes through during puberty. In this chapter, we're going to get into more detail, especially about the stuff girls go through. So let's talk vaginas! Vaginas are amazing, and to have one, in my opinion, is an honor. On pages 62–67, you'll find a vocabulary list and diagrams of what a girl's reproductive system looks like to help you understand what's going on inside your body and what you might see on the outside of your body. It's important to know what your parts look like, because they are uniquely yours, and you should learn to appreciate all of your body. Since it's kind of hard to see what's going on down there, the best way to look at your own vagina is to hold a hand mirror between your legs and look at the reflection.

I hope the pictures and the vocabulary list help create some clarity about your parts. If you have more questions, don't hesitate to speak with your trusted, knowledgeable adult (TKA). In fact, I recommend using the diagram and word list to start a conversation.

No one should ever ask to see your private parts unless it's a doctor who has asked for permission to conduct a health-and-wellness checkup. If you ever feel uncomfortable about someone asking to see your genitals, tell your TKA. Your body is your body, and it is up to you to decide who can see it.

How many holes do I have down there?

There are two holes located in the vulva. (The vulva is your external genital area, which lots of people just call the "vagina.") There's a smaller hole called the urethra, through which you pee, and a larger hole called the vagina. During your period, blood comes out of your vagina, and it's also the hole through which babies are born. We also all have a butthole, or anus, but that's not a part of your reproductive system, even though it's in the same area.

Which hole does the baby come out of?

A baby comes out of your vagina. If an egg and sperm meet in the fallopian tube, they join together to become a fertilized egg. That egg then travels through the fallopian tube to the uterus, also known as the womb. (This is where the baby will develop, not in the stomach, which is an entirely different organ.) After a time, the fertilized egg implants itself in the uterine lining, where it will grow and develop into an embryo, then a fetus, then a baby over the course of nine months. The uterus is connected to the vagina, but there's a sort of gateway between them called the cervix. When the baby's ready to be born, the cervix opens up, and the baby comes out through the vagina.

Female Anatomy

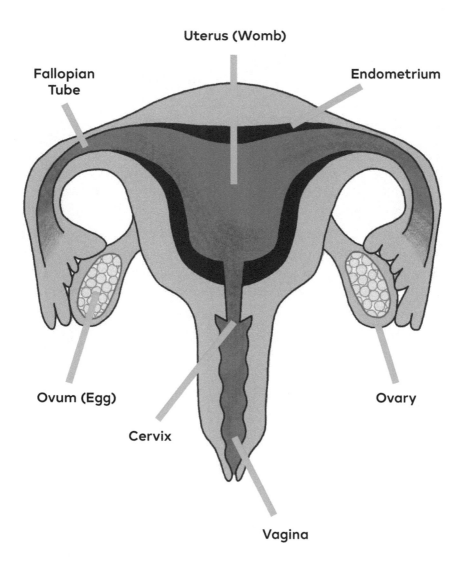

Uterus (Womb)

Fallopian Tube

Endometrium

Ovum (Egg)

Cervix

Ovary

Vagina

ANUS   It's not part of the reproductive system, but often people think of the anus as a "hole down there." It's actually a part of your digestive system, and it's where bowel movements (aka poop) leave the body.

CERVIX   This is the very bottom part of your uterus, and it leads into your vagina. It's a very important part of your reproductive system, as it's kind of like the door that keeps the baby in the uterus while it develops.

CLITORIS   This is one of my favorite body parts, because it's the part of the female genitals that exists only for pleasurable sensations. It's built kind of like a penis, with a head (glans) and a shaft. But unlike the penis, the shaft of the clitoris is inside the body, and only the glans is visible. It has about eight thousand nerve endings, which can cause a lot of sensation when stimulated.

DISCHARGE   Discharge is any fluid that comes out of the body—in this case, out of your vagina. The term is sometimes used to describe the normal secretions of the vagina or any abnormal secretions that can come from an infection of the vagina.

FALLOPIAN TUBES   These are two tubes that extend from the uterus toward the ovaries. I like to think of them as the highway for the egg cell, because when the egg cell (ovum) is fertilized, it travels from the ovary through a fallopian tube to the uterus, where it eventually grows into a baby.

FIMBRIAE   Fimbriae are the tiny, fingerlike fringes on the edges of the fallopian tubes that sweep the ovum from the ovary into the fallopian tube. I think one of the coolest things about the female reproductive system is that the fallopian tubes are not directly connected to the ovaries. So when the eggs leave the ovary, they float free for a while until they get swept into the fallopian tube by the fimbriae.

GENITALS   This is a general term for both male and female reproductive organs, especially the parts on the outside of the body, like the vulva or the penis.

HYMEN   The hymen is a thin membrane that partly covers the opening to the vagina in many females. It looks different for all women, and some women are born without one at all. It may stretch or tear to create a larger opening in the vagina, but it never fully goes away.

LABIA   These are the folds of skin in the female genitals that surround the opening to the urethra and vagina. You have two different sets. First there are the **labia minora**, the smaller, inner set of labia right next to the opening of the vagina, and then there are the **labia majora**, the larger, outer set of labia, which can vary in thickness. Some women's labia minora show, while for others, the outer labia are large enough to cover the inner labia. It's also completely normal if one of your labia is larger, longer, or thicker than the others. No two sets of labia are alike!

MONS PUBIS   The mons pubis is the rounded fatty tissue beneath the skin, lying just beneath the lower abdomen or tummy and above the vulva. During puberty, you will notice hair starting to form there. That is what's called "pubic hair."

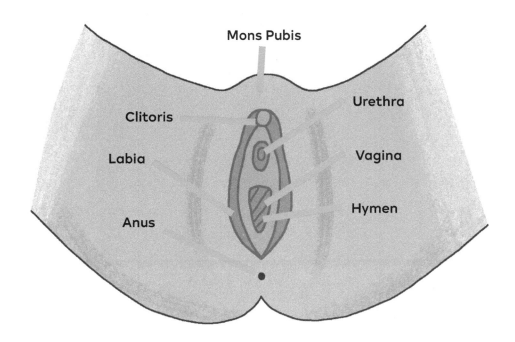

Mons Pubis

Clitoris

Urethra

Labia

Vagina

Anus

Hymen

ORGASM   The physical and emotional sensation experienced at the peak of sexual excitement, usually resulting from the stimulation of sexual organs.

OVARY   The organ that stores ova (egg cells) and produces female hormones. You have two ovaries, one on each side of your uterus.

OVUM   The female sex cell, sometimes called the egg cell or just the egg. Women are born with all our eggs—about two million of them—already in our ovaries, but by the time you hit puberty, many of them have died off, and you have about 400,000 to 500,000 eggs. When one of those eggs gets fertilized by a sperm, it can grow into a baby.

PERINEUM   The area between the anus and vulva on a girl (or between the anus and scrotum on a boy).

PREPUCE   Also known as the "clitoral hood," this is the skin surrounding and protecting the head of the clitoris.

PUBERTY   This is the process you're probably going through right now! It's the time in your life when you're maturing into an adult.

PUBIC HAIR   Hair that often grows around the male and female genitals during puberty. Pubic hair can be similar or different in texture or color to a person's head and body hair.

REPRODUCTION   The act of replicating or making more of something; human reproduction means producing more humans, aka making a baby.

SEXUAL AND REPRODUCTIVE ANATOMY   These are the parts of male and female bodies that are involved in reproduction as well as giving and receiving sexual pleasure and intimate physical contact.

URETHRA   The tube that carries urine from the bladder out of the body, in both males and females. In males, the urethra is inside the penis. In females, it's just above the vagina. The **urethral opening** is the opening of the urethra to the outside of the body.

UTERUS   Also known as the womb, the uterus is a pear-shaped organ with a muscular wall and lining, where the fetus develops if a woman becomes pregnant. The lining of the uterus is what a woman sheds during her period.

VAGINA   The tube-like organ that connects the uterus to the outside of the body. It's also the hole through which blood comes during your period, and where a penis goes in during vaginal sex.

VAGINAL OPENING   The opening of the vagina to the outside of the body.

VULVA   The external area of the female sexual and reproductive anatomy, including the labia and clitoris. Technically, because the vagina is on the inside of your body, what you see in the mirror is your vulva, not your vagina.

What is a period?
Why do we get our periods?

Getting your period (menstruating) is an important part of how our bodies make babies. Every month, an egg cell (ovum) is released from one of a woman's ovaries. If she has sex with a man, his sperm can fertilize the egg. Then the fertilized egg implants in the uterus, where it grows into a baby. The uterus is lined with special nutritious material that helps the baby grow. But if a woman doesn't get pregnant, the uterus has to get rid of that lining so it can grow a new one in case next month's egg does get fertilized.

Think of it like hotel bedsheets—every time a person checks out of a hotel room, housekeeping services take the sheets off the bed and put on new ones for the next guest. Your uterus is like a hotel for your eggs. If the egg doesn't meet a sperm, it checks out of the hotel, and the uterus sheds its lining. That lining leaves your body through your vagina, along with some blood and the unfertilized egg (which is too tiny to see). That's what your period is. If you get pregnant, the uterus actually uses the lining, and you don't get your period again until after the baby is born.

When should I get my period?

Most girls get their first period at the beginning of puberty, around ages 10 to 14. The average age is 12, but everyone is different. When you start having your period, that means your body is mature enough to make a baby, but it doesn't mean your mind or emotions are ready to have a baby. When you get older, usually between 48 and 55 years old, you'll stop having your period. That's called "menopause," and it means your body can't make babies anymore. It's important to remember that during the first few years of puberty, your menstrual cycle may not be regular. Your period may only last a few days, or it may come after 35 days instead of 28. A few girls don't get their periods at all, due to a variety of reasons. For example, some girls are born with a vagina but don't have a functioning uterus, while trans girls don't have a uterus at all.

What is the correct way to use a pad?

When you have blood coming out of your vagina during your period, you need a way to absorb that blood. Most women use pads and/or tampons. Pads come with adhesive material on the back, just like a sticker you'd put in a notebook. To use a pad, place it sticky-side down on your panties, and wrap the "wings" around the material of your panties to secure it in place. When it's full of blood, throw it away and replace it with a clean one. Pads come in different shapes, sizes, and absorbencies. If you have a heavy flow with a lot of blood, you'll need a more absorbent pad. If you have a light flow, you can use a thinner one. They even make extra-absorbent pads to wear while you're sleeping. While you're getting used to your period, I recommend keeping an extra pair of pads and underwear in your locker or bag. I can speak from experience when I say that sometimes your period will pop up on you, and if you don't have any pads on hand, it'll be a messy situation. Always remember: Proper planning prevents problematic periods.

How do I use a tampon?

Tampons are another popular way to absorb menstrual blood. Instead of sitting on your underwear like a pad, a tampon is a small piece of cotton or other material that you insert directly into your vagina. Contrary to what some people might tell you, using a tampon does *not* take away your virginity, and it will *not* stretch out your vagina or make it loose. To use one, follow the instructions on the box to put it inside your vagina. When you're first learning to use them, you may find it helpful to lie down or place one foot up on the toilet while putting it in. When it's full of blood, you take it out, throw it away, and insert a new one. Even if you're not bleeding very heavily, it's important to remember to change your tampon every four hours, because if they stay in too long they can give you an infection. It's also important to remember that anything going into your vagina needs to be clean, so don't set an unwrapped tampon down on any surface before you insert it.

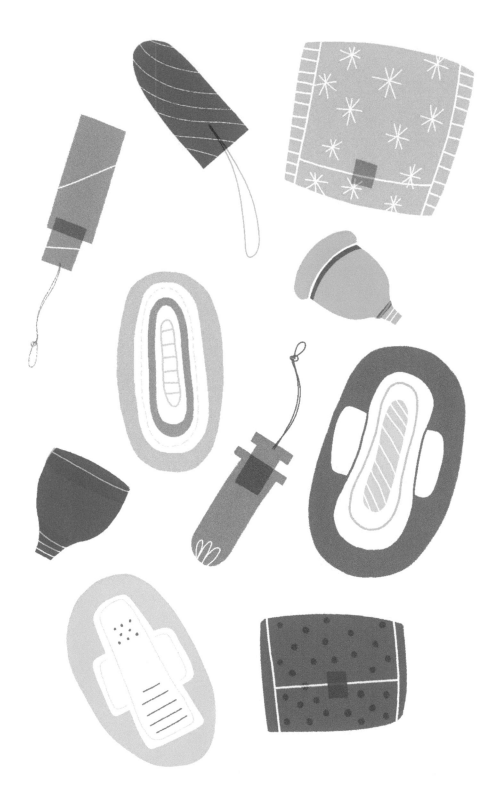

What other things do people use for their periods besides pads and tampons?

Disposable pads and tampons are the most popular choices, but there are other options too, including washable cloth pads, very thin pads called panty liners, and disposable or reusable menstrual cups, which you insert into your vagina and empty out every few hours. If you have questions, ask your trusted, knowledgeable adult and/or a doctor about what options there are.

How much blood comes out when I'm on my period?

Surprisingly, not much at all. It often seems like a lot, even to adult women, but the amount of blood is usually 2 to 4 tablespoons over the course of five to seven days. If you see clumps or clots of blood, don't worry. That's the lining from the walls of your uterus, which your uterus sheds during your period. All of this is totally normal. If your period tends to last longer than seven days, you should talk to your trusted, knowledgeable adult and maybe even your doctor to ensure you're having a healthy period.

What's the normal amount of pain to feel during your period?

All women experience pain differently during different parts of their menstrual cycle. The most common kind is cramps in your lower abdomen leading up to and during your period. That's your uterus contracting as it sheds its lining, which is the red, blood-like substance that comes out of your vagina during your period. Sometimes you may also experience lower back pain, breast tenderness, and headaches. The severity of the pain varies from person to person. Usually it's manageable, but some people experience pretty severe pain. If you find the pain interrupts your day-to-day activities, sleep schedule, or ability to eat, then talk to your parents or another trusted, knowledgeable adult. Doctors can help find treatments to reduce the symptoms of your cramps, including taking birth control.

How long will my period last?

Usually five to seven days, but it is different for everyone. You might have a short, five-day period one month, and a long, ten-day period the next month, especially during puberty, when your menstrual cycle is more irregular. Hormonal birth control can change how long your periods last and how heavy they are. Some hormonal birth control types can take your period away completely while you're on them. Others can make you have your period every three months instead of every month.

What happens when a woman gets her tubes tied?

Your fallopian tubes are like freeways between your ovaries (where your eggs, or ova, are housed) and your uterus (where a fertilized egg grows into a baby). They provide a perfect environment for a sperm to fertilize an egg, which then continues down the fallopian freeway to implant itself in the uterus and grow into a baby. When a woman "gets her tubes tied," nothing is actually tied into a knot. A doctor uses surgery to block the tubes, shutting down the fallopian freeway so that sperm and eggs can't meet and a woman can't get pregnant.

Why do I have white stuff in my panties?

That white stuff is called "discharge," and it's something your body naturally produces as part of your menstrual cycle. If you notice a slippery discharge that looks kind of like egg whites, it probably means you're ovulating. Ovulation is the time when your body has released an egg and you're fertile, meaning that if you have sex, you can get pregnant. The discharge helps create a friendly environment for sperm to meet egg and make a baby. If it's thicker and white in color, that's also normal. And it's also normal to have some brown discharge after your period. If the discharge is excessive, itchy, clumpy, or smells funny, talk to your trusted, knowledgeable adult and see a doctor. You may be experiencing an infection.

Why do I sometimes smell down there?

Vaginas come with smells. Your whole body has its own unique smell, and your vagina is no different. It's perfectly normal to sniff your panties to get to know your smell—in fact, I encourage it. How will you know if something's wrong with your vagina's smell if you don't know what it smells like when everything's right? The aroma should be distinct but relatively mild and not unpleasant. It will also smell different during different times of your menstrual cycle. During your period, for example, it often smells like iron, metal, or pennies. If you notice a strong, unpleasant, or fishy odor, you might have an infection. But on the other hand, your vagina shouldn't smell like a flower or a fruit, because it's neither of those. It's a vagina! So don't use any douche products or perfumes on it. They can mess up your vagina's self-cleaning process and give you an infection—and that definitely won't smell good.

How do I wash my private area?

When you're in the shower or bath, you want to be sure to allow warm water to run over the vulva and labia (the parts of your genitals that are on the outside of your body). Open your lips to allow water to run over your vagina. It's important to understand that throughout the day your natural discharge, panty fuzz, and skin cells can get caught in the folds of your labia and create a substance known as smegma. Make sure to remove all of that, and don't be afraid to look at your vagina to ensure it's all gone. You can use a mild, unscented soap on your vulva, but you should never use any soap of any kind inside the opening of your vagina. It keeps itself clean, and putting soap inside it can mess up the chemical balance and cause an infection.

What should I do if I get an infection?

There are many different types of infections we can get "down there," like yeast infections, urinary tract infections (UTIs), bacterial vaginosis (BV), and, if you're sexually active, sexually transmitted infections (STIs). If you notice pain, itching, bad smells, or more discharge than usual in your vaginal area, you may have an infection. Dealing with an infection on our own can be tricky because we are not doctors. There are a lot of websites that will give you information on signs and symptoms, and those websites can be helpful. But if you think you might have an infection, you need to talk to your parent or trusted, knowledgeable adult, and seek medical attention. You don't want to put off speaking with someone, or the infection might become something more serious than it already is. If you're embarrassed to talk about it in front of your parents, by this time in your life, it is possible that your doctor will ask your parent to leave the room. The doctor's office is a completely safe place to ask questions, and you can tell your doctor about any issues you may be having.

When do I need to get a bra?

Bras are created to support your breasts. If you can see your breast buds or nipples underneath a T-shirt, or if you feel like they're moving all over the place, it's probably time for a training bra. Do not be afraid to talk to a trusted, knowledge-able adult woman about your boobies! When you go shopping for bras, be sure to try on a bunch of different ones to see what's most comfortable. All women's bodies are different, and breasts come in all different shapes and sizes. During puberty, boobs don't always grow at the same time, so one might be bigger than the other. Don't worry, this is totally normal, and eventually they'll more or less even out (though even as an adult woman, your boobs might still be slightly different sizes). No one is perfectly symmetrical.

Why are my boobs sore?

When you're going through puberty, your body is changing and growing. First you grow breast buds, which grow into full breasts over time. As your boobs grow, they might feel heavy, tender to the touch, or even itchy. This is all normal! The pain will lessen as you move into adolescence and adulthood, although even as an adult, you might still experience some tenderness during your menstrual cycle. Being physically active can help reduce tenderness, but it's important to have the right sports bra to support your boobs. Support is the key!

Why am I starting to get dimples on my thighs?

Welcome to womanhood, honey! Those dimples are cellulite, which is a fancy way of saying "a bunch of fat cells under your skin." Most women have cellulite, no matter how skinny or athletic they are. It does have a purpose, so don't freak out. Your body needs a certain amount of fat to maintain healthy growth and development into womanhood. From this point forward, your body will hold on to more fat in certain areas such as your breasts, hips, butt, and thighs because your body will need that fat if you ever decide to get pregnant. Love your body, your lady lumps, and all your wonderful curves. There's no reason to worry about cellulite when we almost all have it!

I hate my boobs and my periods and sometimes I wish I was a boy. Am I transgender or gay or what?

As a cisgender woman, there have been times in my life when I wished I was a boy, hated my boobs, and dreaded my monthly period. However, I never had the feeling of knowing I was really a boy or identifying as transgender. Considering the amount of changes your body is going through right now, it can sometimes seem like being a boy would be much easier, but remember, they're going through a lot of changes too. Just because you sometimes get frustrated about having boobs or getting your period does not necessarily mean you're trans. I would recommend you talk to your trusted, knowledgeable adult about these feelings. Whether you're trans or cis, gay or straight, you're you, and you're awesome.

♥ When you were my age did you have a trusted, knowledgeable adult you could talk to?

♥ Do you remember when you started your period (or when the girls your age started their periods)?

♥ Have you ever had an embarrassing moment with your body that you can tell me about?

chapter **4**

Healthy Relationships

Relationships of all kinds are important to your life today and will continue to be important through-out the rest of your life. As you get older, you'll start learning what you value in your relationships, no matter whether they're friendships, family relationships, or romantic relationships. I think it's important for you to speak with a family member or other trusted adult about what they value in a good relationship. Personally, I hold honesty, trust, and nonjudgment high on my values list when it comes to the relationships in my life.

Why is my family so hard on me?

Your parents might sometimes be hard on you while you're growing up, but usually they mean well. Your family probably wants what's best for you, and now that you're maturing and changing your perspective on the world, you're at the very beginning of the transition to a time when you'll be able to decide what's best for yourself. That can create conflict between you and your parents. It's a normal part of growing up, and the best way to handle it is to talk honestly with your parents about your feelings.

How can I become more popular?

Popularity is subjective. If you like the people you kick it with and they like you, you're popular enough. As long as you focus on loving yourself, working toward your goals, and being kind and respectful to others, you'll always have enough friends— maybe not in middle school or high school, but later on in life. It's very common for people who weren't at all popular in school to gain a lot of friends and have a great social life when they grow up.

Is everyone else having fun without me?

It's a very normal, common feeling to worry that others are having fun without you. Even adults worry about it some-times too! But the truth is that comparing your life to others' lives is a waste of time. All it does is distract you from living your best life and achieving your goals. When you watch people's lives on social media, you're not getting a true depic-tion of the whole story. You're just getting all the good stuff that they choose to share and none of the bad stuff that they keep to themselves. The people who seem to have picture-perfect lives on Snapchat or Instagram are often just as worried as you are that they're being left out.

Why am I so stressed all the time?

Puberty is a unique challenge for both you and your parents. Your body, brain, and emotions are going through a lot of changes, plus your workload at school is probably intensifying. You might feel like you're under a lot of pressure from your parents, teachers, classmates, friends, and even yourself. It's important to keep in mind that some level of stress is healthy and will help push your life and achievements to the next level. But too much stress is unhealthy for your mind and body. To keep your stress level manageable, make sure you get enough sleep, eat a balanced diet, and talk to your trusted, knowledgeable adult about your feelings on a regular basis. Keeping a journal can be very useful too. It's helpful to identify activities that make you feel good, like dancing, reading, or playing sports, and create time for those activities. Meditation and mindfulness can also help reduce stress by creating time to unplug.

Why do people gossip about me?

The short answer is: 'Cause haters are gonna hate. Often-times, when someone talks about you behind your back, they're jealous of something you're doing and attempting to fill a void in their own life, or maybe they're just bored. They might also be mad at you but too afraid to discuss it with you directly. Remember, it's usually best to just be honest and talk with someone about your feelings, instead of gossiping about it to others. And if someone gossips about you to others, it reflects badly on that person, not on you.

What do I say when my partner or friends make fun of me?

If people are making fun of you, it's a clear indicator that those people are shady. I can't tell you the exact words to use, but I can stress that you must clearly communicate that you won't tolerate being disrespected. It's important to set boundaries in all of your relationships. A boundary is the baseline of how you want to be treated. If someone keeps crossing your boundaries even when you've made them clear, then you can spend less time with them until they learn to respect your boundaries. It's also important for you to respect others' boundaries and not treat them in ways they don't like.

How can I stop being bullied (or cyberbullied)?

A bully is a person who uses their power to intimidate you, hurt you, or try to force you to do something you don't want to do. With social media the way it is, it's easier than ever for bullies to attack others. Whether they're bullying you at school, in a public place, or online, bullies use words, actions, and the Internet to psychologically harass and abuse you. You should never act this way toward others, and if someone acts this way toward you, you should immediately speak to your trusted, knowledgeable adult about the situation. I want to really stress that this is not a matter you should keep to yourself. Emotional distress or pain is just as serious, if not more so, than physical pain. It's not snitching if you ask for help with bullying; it is self-care and self-love.

If a boy bothers me, does it mean he has a crush on me?

When we're young, we're not always prepared to communicate our feelings to other people, and as a result, people sometimes give their crushes negative attention instead of positive attention. This is especially true for boys, who tend to mature a little more slowly than girls. If a boy keeps teasing you or calling you names, it might mean he has a crush on you, or it might not. What's important is that it's not okay for anyone to be mean to you, even if they're doing it because they like you, and you don't have to put up with it.

How do I know if someone has a crush on me?

If someone has a crush on you, they'll probably pay extra attention to you. They might seem nervous around you, talk to or text you more, chat with you on social media, compliment you, or do nice things for you. If you're crushing on the same person who's crushing on you, that's great! But just because someone likes you doesn't mean you have to like them back. You never owe anyone a date, and you can always say no to anyone who asks you out, even if they treat you nicely.

How do you make your crush like you without changing who you are?

You can't make anyone like anyone else, but no crush is worth changing your awesome self! Any crush worthy of your time is into you just the way you are. At the end of the day, no one—crush or otherwise—is worth you feeling like you need to change who you are. If they don't like you the way you are, they don't need to be your crush or take up space in your life.

What should I expect in a relationship? What qualifies as a good relationship?

This is a time in your life when you're starting to explore new and different types of relationships, including romantic ones. It's hard for me to explain exactly what you should expect in a relationship, because a relationship should be defined by the people in it, but honesty, trust, acceptance, respect, communication, and support are the keys to any good relationship.

In a healthy relationship, people view each other in a positive light and encourage each other to be their best selves every day. They enjoy and celebrate each other's abilities, personalities, and achievements, and can talk to each other honestly, trusting that they will be heard, not ignored or attacked. When you're feeling down or sad, a good partner has a way of speaking to you that builds you up and makes your confidence soar. And last but not least, you want to be with someone you can have fun with, who makes you laugh. I know that right now you might be thinking relationships should come with some sort of physical stuff like kissing or holding hands, and they definitely can, but that doesn't always need to be the case. Intimacy is something that's not just physical but also emotional.

How to Recognize Unhealthy Relationships

Here is a snapshot of something I use with my students to help them understand the characteristics of an unhealthy relationship. If you notice that your relationship has any of these characteristics, you should speak with your trusted, knowledgeable adult (TKA) to reevaluate the relationship and the person you're dealing with. Your safety is the most important thing, and now that you're growing up, it's time to learn the signs of an unhealthy or abusive relationship. Even if you're not in a relationship, you should review the Power and Control Wheel with your TKA and discuss what a healthy relationship looks like to them. Your TKA will be able to help you identify what should be happening in your relationships, and that goes for friendships as well as romantic relationships.

VIOLENCE

Sexual

TEEN POWER & CONTROL WHEEL

Peer Pressure
Threatening to expose another's weakness or spread rumors. Telling malicious lies about another to peer group.

Anger/ Emotional Abuse
Putting others down. Making others feel badly, name calling. Making others feel crazy. Playing mind games. Humiliating others, making others feel guilty.

Isolation/ Exclusion Controlling what another does, who they see and talk to, what they read, where they go. Limiting outside involvement. Using jealousy to justify actions.

Using Social Status Treating the other like a servant. Making all the decisions. Acting like the "master of the castle," being the one to define men's and women's roles.

Sexual Coercion
Manipulation or making threats to get sex. Getting her pregnant. Threatening to take the children away. Getting someone drunk or drugged to have sex.

Intimidation
Making someone afraid by using looks, actions, gestures. Smashing things. Destroying property. Abusing pets. Displaying weapons.

Threats
Making and/or carrying out threats to hurt another. Threatening to leave, to commit suicide, to report the other to the police. Making the other drop charges or do illegal things.

Minimize/ Deny/Blame
Making light of the abuse. Not taking concerns about it seriously. Saying it didn't happen. Shifting responsibility for abusive behavior. Saying the other caused it.

Physical

Sexual

VIOLENCE

Adapted from http://www.ncdsv.org/images/Teen%20P&C%20wheel%20NO%20SHADING.pdf.

What are red flags for an unhealthy or abusive relationship?

If someone tries to change you or make you feel like you're not good enough the way you are, that's an unhealthy relationship. A good partner doesn't lie to you, belittle you, or try to control what you do. If they try to justify those kinds of actions by saying they're jealous, don't buy it. There is no room for jealousy in healthy, supportive relationships. Threats are also high on my list of red flags. No one should threaten you in any way, including threatening to harm themselves if you don't do what they want you to do. And it is never, ever acceptable for someone to physically harm you or to pressure or force you to do sexual stuff you don't want to do. Your body is your body, which means you have the right to choose what to do or not do with it. If you notice any of these red flags, you should talk with your trusted, knowledgeable adult about ways to end unhealthy relationships. You do not deserve to be treated badly, and it is not your fault, no matter who you are or what you've done. You deserve to be with someone who doesn't harm you emotionally or physically.

Is it normal that my partner tells me who to hang out with?

Heck no! A partner who tells you who you can hang out with is a partner who is trying to control you. In a healthy relationship, you have your own life outside of your partner, and that includes the ability to choose your friends.

Should I give my social media passwords to my partner to prove I like them?

Nope! Anyone who is trying to control your whereabouts or access to your private accounts—even if they say they're only trying to look out for you or that it will prove you love them—is someone who does not have your best interests in mind. Remember, one of the pillars of a healthy relationship is trust. Whether you're single or in a relationship, you are entitled to your privacy, and people in a relationship do not need to tell each other their passwords.

How do I break up with someone?

If you're thinking of breaking up with someone, it can be helpful to make a list of reasons why the relationship is not working (write it down!) and review it with your trusted, knowledgeable adult. But you don't need a "reason" to break up with someone. Not wanting to be in a relationship with them anymore is enough reason to break up, even if they're treating you well. It's enough to say, "My feelings have changed, and I want to break up." Your TKA can give you more pointers on what to say and how to end a relationship. It's often hard to do something you know will hurt someone else's feelings, but you're both young, and I promise you will both get over it and go on to date other people. If you're going to break up with someone, I recommend being clear about your decision. You don't want to be going back and forth, breaking up and getting back together again—it just makes the process harder on everyone. Remember, breakups can be difficult, no matter who dumps whom. It's totally normal for you to feel sadness and grief for a while after you dump someone.

How do I get over being dumped?

No matter who dumps whom, with breakups come sadness and grief. You're going to feel those feelings for a while no matter what, but there are some steps you can take to work through them. I know it will be hard, but it's best to put your phone down and unplug from the person you just broke up with. If you need to, block them from your social media. Turn to your support system—your parents or other trusted adults, your friends, even your pets—and try to fill your time with activities that make you feel good. You can think of it as kind of dating yourself. Remember, your first and most important relationship is always the one you have with yourself.

What do I do if I like my best friend's ex?

I can tell you what not to do: Don't secretly start seeing your friend's ex behind their back. Instead, put yourself in your best friend's shoes. How long ago did they break up? Why did they break up? Is your friend still feeling grief over the end of the relationship? If so, you should probably try to find someone else to have a crush on. If you think it's worth it to pursue the possibility of a relationship with her ex, you can talk to your friend about it, but keep it real and be honest. And be aware that the conversation might not go well.

Why can't there be more than two people in a relationship?

Being in a romantic relationship with more than one person is called polyamory. That could mean three people are in a relationship together, or that two people in a relationship are also dating other people on the side, or some combination of the two. There is nothing wrong with polyamory, as long as everyone involved is aware of what's going on and is okay with engaging in a relationship with more than one other person. Here's the thing: Being in a relationship with only one other person is already very complex. Being in a polyamorous relationship is even more complex, and it requires a lot of advanced communication and relationship skills that even many adults don't have. I personally don't have the time or emotional availability to be in a relationship with more than one partner at a time, and I write about this kind of stuff for a living! The bottom line is that if you know some adults who are in a polyamorous relationship, there's nothing wrong with that, but if you want to try it out, you should probably wait until you're older and have learned more about how to be in a romantic relationship first.

What do I do if my partner asks me to text them naked pictures?

The first thing you need to know is that although you have the right to do what you want with your body, because you are under 18, there are laws against sending naked pictures of yourself to anyone. Until you're both over 18, you and your partner could get in very serious legal trouble for sending or receiving nudes. Second, consider that we live in a world where people love to overshare, and remember that what is put online often can't be erased. Even if you trust your partner not to show your nudes to anyone else, accidents happen. Their phone could get hacked, or a computer-repair person could accidentally stumble across the photos. Even after you're 18, think about the potential consequences. If you still feel compelled, be smart. Don't include your face or any identifiable markers (tattoos, piercings, birthmarks, etc.) in the photo.

♥ What can I do to feel like I fit in?

♥ What characteristics should I look for in my friends and romantic partners?

♥ How would you suggest I express my feelings to people I am interested in?

♥ What's it feel like to be in love?

chapter 5

Let's Talk about Sex

Puberty is the time in our lives when we become sexually mature, meaning our bodies become ready and able to have sex and make babies. You're probably starting to become very curious about sex, wondering how exactly it works and why people do it. This chapter will answer some of the questions you have, and maybe even a few you didn't know you had. But don't just rely on this book. Before you engage in sex, you should speak with your trusted, knowledgeable adult.

What is a virgin?
What does it mean to
"lose your virginity"?

Simply put, a virgin is a person who has never had sex. However, sex is not simple; it's complex and personal. There once was a time when virginity was only spoken of in the context of a penis penetrating a vagina. But sex is defined by the people engaging in the activity. Furthermore, some people are not into penis/vagina sex, but that is not to say they will never lose their "virginity."

It is important to remember that when it comes to sexual activity, getting pregnant is not the only risk. When you think about "losing your virginity," think about the forms of sexual activity that come with risks. There are three main sexual acts that, if not done using protection, carry the highest risks of STIs (sexually transmitted infections), HIV, and pregnancy. These acts include oral sex (mouth on genitals), anal sex (penis in anus), and vaginal sex (penis in vagina). Of course, there are risks associated with sexual activity beyond oral, vaginal, and anal sex, but the risk of infection is lower with other forms of sexual activity. Before becoming sexually active in any way, I urge you to discuss it with your trusted, knowledgeable adult as well as your partner, to review the level of risk and what steps you can take to reduce any risks associated with sexual behavior.

What happens during sex?

The most common definition of sex (also referred to as "sexual intercourse") is when a penis enters a vagina. However, there are also other forms of sex, like oral sex, where one person puts their mouth on their partner's genitals, or anal sex, where a penis penetrates an anus. All of these are ways that people have sex. They can all come with the risk of contracting a sexually transmitted infection, but vaginal sex is the only way you can get pregnant.

What Is Birth Control?

Birth control is a term used to describe the act of preventing pregnancy before it begins. The various ways women use birth control may be different, although no matter the method, birth control is a way for women to take control of their health and family-planning needs. There are different types of birth control, some of which are more effective than others, and not all methods will work for all people. It's important to remember that the only sure way to prevent unplanned pregnancy and the risk of STIs is abstinence, which is the term used for refraining from sexual intercourse. The easiest way to think about the different methods of birth control is to put them in four major categories: barrier methods, hormonal methods, the rhythm method, and emergency contraceptives.

I want to be sure you are armed with as much information as possible so you can find the method that will be best for you, so I have broken them down by category.

BARRIER METHODS   Barrier methods of birth control work just like they sound; they create a "barrier" that prevents sperm from entering the uterus or fallopian tubes where fertilization takes place. Condoms and diaphragms are among the most common barrier methods of birth control. Unlike the other methods below, these are used during the act of intercourse.

HORMONAL METHODS   These methods use medications that work by introducing synthetic hormones, which act like progesterone and estrogen, to alter the body's natural hormones to create a kind of trifecta of protection that impacts the three important factors in becoming pregnant.

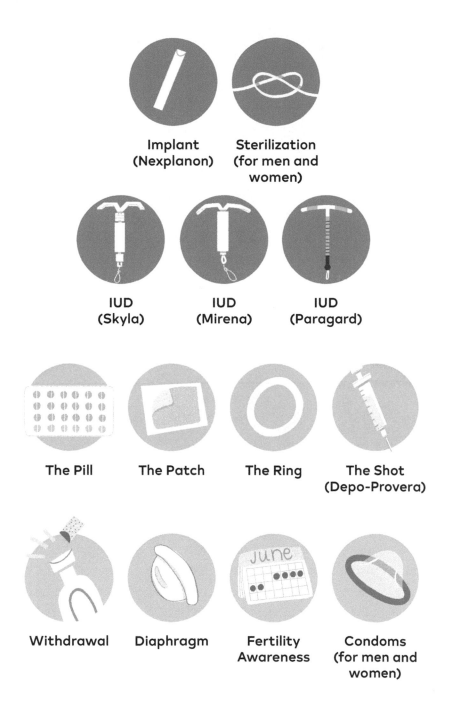

Implant
(Nexplanon)

Sterilization
(for men and
women)

IUD
(Skyla)

IUD
(Mirena)

IUD
(Paragard)

The Pill

The Patch

The Ring

The Shot
(Depo-Provera)

Withdrawal

Diaphragm

Fertility
Awareness

Condoms
(for men and
women)

First, an ovum (egg cell) is released from an ovary; hormonal methods of birth control stop the ovum from being released. Second, for a sperm to get into the uterus it must pass through the cervix; hormonal birth control thickens cervical mucus, which blocks sperm from entering. Third, the impact of the hormones in birth control thins the lining of the uterus, which reduces the likelihood of a fertilized egg implanting in the lining.

All hormonal methods of birth control *must* be prescribed by a doctor. Although these methods were developed to prevent unplanned pregnancy, doctors sometimes prescribe these medications to help with other female health issues, such as irregular periods brought on by polycystic ovarian syndrome (PCOS), or endometriosis, a condition where tissue that is normally inside the uterus grows outside of it, which can make for heavy periods and excessive cramping.

RHYTHM METHOD This method goes by various names, including periodic abstinence, fertility awareness, or natural family planning. Although this method is all-natural, it's not necessarily recommended for teens. The way it works is by monitoring the days of your menstrual cycle that fall in your "fertile window." These are your most fertile days and occur in the middle of your menstrual cycle, usually 12 to 16 days after your period starts each month. Some couples feel that this is the best option. However, while you are a teen and your body's hormones and periods are regulating, it can be challenging to accurately and consistently predict your fertile window. There are a ton of apps available that can help you locate this window, but the method is not an exact science and should not be relied upon while your periods are irregular.

EMERGENCY CONTRACEPTIVES (EC) These are methods that you only use after sex, which is why you may have heard them called "the morning after pill." They work to block pregnancy by using pretty much the same hormones as in regular birth control. They can be used up to five days after you have engaged in intercourse, although it is always best to take the medication as soon after intercourse as possible because the rate of effectiveness drops the longer you wait. If fertilization and implantation have already taken place, emergency contraceptives will not end the pregnancy. I want to be clear that these options are for *emergencies only* and should *not* be considered as a regular birth control method.

These options are all great ways to take control of your family planning, but remember, the only 100-percent-sure way to prevent unplanned pregnancy is to practice abstinence by not engaging in sex. It is also very important to remember that aside from preventing an unplanned pregnancy, there are other things you must consider when thinking about engaging in sex, like STIs. Birth control doesn't protect you from STIs. You can reduce your risk of STI exposure by using condoms correctly and consistently. Remember that condoms work great alongside all other forms of birth control.

Why do people like having sex?

Sex can be a lot of fun! Sexual arousal can be very pleasurable, and at peak arousal, you may have an orgasm, which releases a chemical called oxytocin in your brain that makes you feel really good. Sex can also be enjoyable because it involves being intimate with a romantic partner you care about, but you don't necessarily need another person around. Masturbation is a way to enjoy the physical pleasure of sex even if you're not ready to do it with another person.

What happens when people get sexually aroused?

Knowing what's happening when you get aroused can help you make safer decisions, because you can control your body instead of your body controlling you. When you become aroused, your brain and your vagina are communicating with each other. This is known as the human sexual response cycle, and it's a four-stage process.

STAGE 1 Excitement. Your nipples get hard, your heart beats faster, you'll feel warmth in your genitals, and your vagina will produce more wetness. This excitement phase can last anywhere from minutes to hours.

STAGE 2 Plateau. This is a continuation of excitement. If you think of arousal like a roller coaster, the plateau is when the roller coaster reaches the top of the hill.

STAGE 3 Orgasm. This is the climax of sexual arousal. This is like the thrilling part of the roller coaster when you reach the top of the hill and zoom down the other side. Your muscles tighten, your vagina squeezes or pulses, and you might get a warm, tingling feeling all over your body. (For men, orgasm is when the penis ejaculates semen.)

STAGE 4 Resolution. During this phase, your body calms down and returns to normal. While in the resolution phase, your genitals can be very sensitive, and continued stimulation might feel too intense or even slightly painful.

What does sex do for people?

Sex can do different things for different people. It can even do different things for the same person at different times. People enter into sexual experiences for a variety of reasons. Sometimes the goal of sex is create a child, sometimes it's to intimately bond with a partner, and sometimes it's just to feel good.

How are babies made?

When a man and a woman have sex without a barrier method of birth control, the man's penis ejaculates semen into the woman's vagina. The semen contains millions of sperm, which travel through the vagina up to the woman's fallopian tubes. If a woman is ovulating, there might be an egg in the fallopian tubes. If a sperm meets that egg, they will join to become a fertilized egg. The fertilized egg travels down into the uterus, where it implants itself in the uterine lining and develops into a fetus. This can also happen through artificial insemination (when a woman has semen injected into her uterus without having sex) or in vitro fertilization (when an egg is fertilized outside the body in a lab, then implanted into the uterus). The fetus, if taken to full term, gradually grows into a baby. It takes about 40 weeks for this process to happen. It's a huge responsibility to carry a fetus to full term, and after the baby is born, there's the even greater responsibility of motherhood.

Can I get pregnant if a guy pulls out?

Absolutely! It's a common misconception that if you have vaginal sex but the man ejaculates outside the vagina, the woman can't get pregnant. This is untrue. A man can release approximately 100 million sperm cells in a single ejaculation, and technically it only takes one sperm to fertilize an egg. If a guy doesn't pull out very early—or if he gets caught up in the moment and forgets to pull out at all—you can get pregnant. Pre-ejaculate, the fluid that comes out of the penis before ejaculation, may also contain sperm that can get you pregnant, in which case, pulling out wouldn't help at all. Furthermore, pulling out doesn't prevent HIV or other STIs (sexually transmitted infections). That's why it's important to always use a condom.

How does someone know they're pregnant?

There are varying signs that might indicate you're pregnant. The most common one is missing a period. When you're pregnant, your uterus doesn't shed its lining, because that's where the baby is growing. However, during puberty, your period might not be regular yet. Stress, lack of sleep, and an unbalanced diet can also throw your period off. If you have had sex and think you might be pregnant, you can go to any drugstore and buy an over-the-counter pregnancy test. These tests are usually accurate, but not always, so the only way to know for sure whether you're pregnant is to go to a doctor. If you suspect you might be pregnant, it's best you talk to your trusted, knowledgeable adult to seek resources and find places that provide options and counseling.

Does sex hurt?

Sex should feel good overall, but there are times when you may experience some discomfort or slight pain, like if your vagina is not properly lubricated, if it's your first time, or if the condom irritates your skin. Pain during sex could also be caused by an STI (sexually transmitted infection) or a medical condition like vestibulitis. Remember, you don't ever have to continue having sex with someone, even if you've already started, so if you don't like how you're feeling during sex, feel free to stop. If pain during intercourse persists, talk to your trusted, knowledgeable adult, because you might need to see a doctor.

Will my hymen break the first time I have sex?

Most cisgender women are born with a hymen, the thin membrane near the opening of the vagina. Hymens come in all shapes and sizes. A common myth is that having sex for the first time will break your hymen, sometimes called "popping your cherry." Although having sex for the first time may cause your hymen to tear or bleed a little, it doesn't actually "break." And lots of other things can cause that minor tearing even if you've never had sex, like doing splits or riding a bike. Sexual intercourse may change the shape of the hymen, but it never goes away completely.

At what age is it okay to start having sex?

Sex is a serious step in any relationship. It often impacts the mind, body, and emotions of the people involved. In other words, sex can be a big deal! It can be awesome and wonderful, but it can also be difficult, painful, and, quite frankly, scary, especially if you're not ready to deal with all the emotions that come along with sex. If you're not ready to talk about sex with your partner and with your trusted, knowledgeable adult—because if things go wrong, you will need to talk to an adult—you're probably not ready to have sex, even if you have strong feelings for someone. If you and your partner are prepared to accept responsibility for the risks and potential consequences, then you might be ready to start thinking about having sex.

Are other people my age having sex?

Contrary to what you might be seeing, hearing, or feeling, not as many of your peers are having sex as you think. People often talk about "hookup culture" and say that young people are more sexually active these days, but it's not really true. In fact, according to some studies,[4] the average age of first intercourse in the United States is about 17 years old. Don't believe all the hype about hookup culture. When it comes to sex, you should not feel pressure to do it by a certain age. You should do it when you're ready. "Ready" means you're able to communicate with your partner (and your trusted, knowledgeable adult) about your wants and needs, understand potential con- sequences like STIs and unplanned pregnancy, and know what to do to reduce the risk of unwanted outcomes.

Is sex good for your health?

When you're ready, safe, consensual sex (sex you've both said yes to) can provide many benefits to your health and your life. It can create a deeper level of intimacy between two people. It can also relieve stress. However, sexual intercourse comes with responsibilities and potential consequences to your health, like unplanned pregnancy and STIs like HIV. Make sure you always use condoms so that having sex stays helpful, not harmful, for your physical health.

What is abstinence?

If someone is "abstinent" or "practices abstinence," that just means they are choosing not to have sex. As you get older, you can choose whether you want to be abstinent or sexually active. Both are valid choices. One is not better than the other.

What is abortion? Is it bad to have an abortion?

The easiest way to describe abortion is to say simply that it is the ending of a pregnancy; more specifically it means that an embryo or fetus is removed from the uterus (womb). This removal of the fetus happens long before the fetus could survive on its own. Sometimes, this happens naturally in the form of a miscarriage—also known as "spontaneous abortion"—or a woman might decide to intentionally end a pregnancy by taking a medication or having a medical procedure.

The topic of abortion often sparks heated debate, as some people feel that it is wrong to have a procedure that would end a pregnancy at any stage. They are sometime referred to as people who are "pro-life." Other people believe it should be a women's right to choose what is best for her and her body. They are known as people who are "pro-choice." Further still, a lot of people find themselves somewhere in between these two types of people. In 1973, the U.S. Supreme Court handed down the ruling of *Roe v. Wade* that recognized that a woman's right to decide to end her pregnancy is protected under the constitutional right to privacy. Today, there is still much debate about abortion here and elsewhere in the world. Some states in the United States limit access to abortions, and in some countries around the world abortion is illegal. Choosing to have an abortion is a very personal issue that is often impacted by a wide range of outside influences that might include laws, family values, money, religion, or culture. It's best that you speak with your trusted, knowledgeable adult to gain deeper clarity about abortion and the values held by the people that support you. A decision this large is not one I recommend anyone make alone, as you will need support mentally, physically, and emotionally.

What is "safe sex"?

There's no such thing as completely safe sex. The only way to be 100 percent safe is to practice abstinence. Sex always comes with some level of risk, both physically and emotionally. When people talk about safe sex, they're usually talking about using condoms. Of course, there's always a chance the condom will break or something else will go wrong, but condoms are a very important way to reduce the risk of unwanted pregnancy and STIs. But there are other ways to think about safe sex too. For example, I think you can make yourself safer by educating yourself about the risks and responsibilities of sex, getting tested for STIs at the doctor's office, and of course, communicating with your partner. Remember to talk to your trusted, knowledgeable adult about any concerns or questions that you have. They will be able to direct you to the right resources.

What STIs am I at risk for?

If you are engaging in any sexual activity, you're at risk for pretty much all STIs. The types of sexual activity you're engaging in can make the level of risk higher or lower, but at the end of the day, any sexual activity comes with risk.

STIs: What You Need to Know

Sex comes with a lot of possibilities and potential consequences, like pregnancy and sexually transmitted infections
(STIs). STIs, also known as STDs (short for "sexually transmitted diseases") are infections that people can pass to
each other through various sexual acts. Just like you can
catch a cold if you share a drink with someone who has a
cold, you can catch an STI if you have sex with someone
who has an STI. Anyone can get an STI, no matter their age,
gender, or how many times they've had sex. Everybody is at
risk of contracting them, and the only way to protect yourself 100 percent is to practice abstinence. If you're not
abstinent, the easiest, best way to prevent STIs is to use
protection when you have sex. If used correctly, condoms
prevent many STIs *and* unplanned pregnancies.

This chart will give you a brief overview of various STIs and
the health problems they can cause. Review the chart with
your trusted, knowledgeable adult, and ask for more information if you still have questions. Before you start having
sex, you should talk with your partner about how important
it is to have safe sex. Sex is a serious step in any relationship,
and you need to be prepared for all the possibilities.

STI FACTS

CHLAMYDIA

What to Watch For

- Symptoms show up 7–28 days after having sex
- Chlamydia affects women and men
- Most women and some men have no symptoms

Women:

- Discharge from the vagina
- Bleeding from the vagina between periods
- Burning or pain when you urinate
- Need to urinate more often
- Pain in abdomen, sometimes with fever and nausea

Men:

- Watery, white drip from the penis
- Burning or pain when you urinate
- Need to urinate more often
- Swollen or tender testicles

How You Get It

- Spread during vaginal, anal, or oral sex with someone who has chlamydia

If You Don't Get Treated

- You can give chlamydia to your sex partner(s)
- It can lead to more serious infection; reproductive organs can be damaged
- Women and possibly men may no longer be able to have children
- A mother with chlamydia can give it to her baby during childbirth

GONORRHEA

What to Watch For

- Symptoms show up 2–21 days after having sex
- Most women and some men have no symptoms

Women:

- Thick yellow or gray discharge from the vagina
- Burning or pain when you urinate or have a bowel movement
- Abnormal periods or bleeding between periods
- Cramps and pain in the lower abdomen (belly)

Men:

- Thick yellow or greenish drip from the penis
- Burning or pain when you urinate or have a bowel movement
- Need to urinate more often
- Swollen or tender testicles

How You Get It

- Spread during vaginal, anal, or oral sex with someone who has gonorrhea

If You Don't Get Treated

- You can give gonorrhea to your sex partner(s)
- It can lead to more serious infection; reproductive organs can be damaged
- Both men and women may no longer be able to have children
- It can cause heart trouble, skin disease, arthritis, and blindness
- A mother with gonorrhea can give it to her baby in the womb or during childbirth

HEPATITIS B

What to Watch For

- Symptoms show up 1–9 months after contact with the hepatitis B virus
- Many people have no symptoms or mild symptoms
- Flu-like feelings that don't go away
- Tiredness
- Jaundice (yellow skin)
- Dark urine, light-colored bowel movements

How You Get It

- Spread during vaginal, anal, or oral sex with someone who has hepatitis B
- Spread by sharing needles to inject drugs, or for any other reason
- Spread by contact with infected blood

If You Don't Get Treated

- You can give hepatitis B to your sex partner(s) or someone you share a needle with
- Some people recover completely
- Some people cannot be cured: Symptoms go away, but they can still give hepatitis B to others
- It can cause permanent liver damage or liver cancer
- A mother with hepatitis B can give it to her baby during childbirth

HERPES

What to Watch For

- Symptoms show up 1–30 days or longer after having sex
- Many people have no symptoms
- Flu-like feelings
- Small, painful blisters on the sex organs or mouth
- Itching or burning before the blisters appear
- Blisters last 1–3 weeks
- Blisters go away, but you still have herpes; blisters can come back

How You Get It

- Spread during vaginal, anal, or oral sex, and sometimes by genital touching, with someone who has herpes

If You Don't Get Treated

- You can give herpes to your sex partner(s)
- Herpes cannot be cured, but medicine can control it
- A mother with herpes can give it to her baby during childbirth

HIV/AIDS

What to Watch For

- Symptoms show up several months to several years after contact with HIV, the virus that causes AIDS
- It can be present for many years with no symptoms
- Unexplained weight loss or tiredness
- Flu-like feelings that don't go away
- Diarrhea
- White spots in mouth
- In women, yeast infections that don't go away

- **How You Get It**
- Spread during vaginal, anal, or oral sex with someone who has HIV
- Spread by sharing needles to inject drugs, or for any other reason
- Spread by contact with infected blood

If You Don't Get Treated

- You can give HIV to your sex partner(s) or someone you share a needle with
- HIV cannot be cured; it can cause illness and death, but medicines can control it
- A mother with HIV can give it to her baby in the womb, during birth, or while breastfeeding

HPV/GENITAL WARTS

What to Watch For

- Symptoms show up weeks, months, or years after contact with HPV
- Many people have no symptoms
- Some types cause genital warts: Small, bumpy warts on the sex organs and anus
- Itching or burning around the sex organs
- After warts go away, the virus sometimes stays in the body; the warts can come back
- Some types cause cervical cancer in women: Cell changes on the cervix can only be detected by a Pap test from a health-care provider

How You Get It

- Spread during vaginal, anal, or oral sex, and sometimes by genital touching, with someone who has HPV

If You Don't Get Treated

- You can give HPV to your sex partner(s)

- Most HPV goes away on its own in about 2 years

- Warts may go away on their own, remain unchanged, or grow and spread

- A mother with warts can give them to her baby during childbirth

- Some types can lead to cervical cancer if not found and treated

SYPHILIS

What to Watch For

1st Stage:

- Symptoms show up 1–12 weeks after having sex

- A painless sore or sores on the mouth or sex organs

- Sore lasts 2–6 weeks

- Sore goes away, but you still have syphilis

2nd Stage:

- Symptoms show up as the sore heals or after

- A rash anywhere on the body

- Flu-like feelings

- Rash and flu-like feelings go away, but you still have syphilis

How You Get It

- Spread during vaginal, anal, or oral sex, and sometimes by genital touching, with someone who has syphilis

If You Don't Get Treated

- You can give syphilis to your sex partner(s)
- A mother with syphilis can give it to her baby during pregnancy or have a miscarriage
- Can cause heart disease, brain damage, blindness, and death

TRICHOMONIASIS ("TRICH")

What to Watch For

- Symptoms show up 5–28 days after having sex
- Affects both men and women
- Many people have no symptoms

Women:

- Itching, burning, or irritation in the vagina
- Yellow, greenish, or gray discharge form the vagina

Men:

- Watery, white drip from the penis
- Burning or pain when you urinate
- Need to urinate more often

How You Get It

- Spread during vaginal sex

If You Don't Get Treated

- You can give trich to your sex partner(s)
- Uncomfortable symptoms will continue
- Men can get infections in the prostate gland

Adapted from http://pub.etr.org/productdetails.aspx?id=100000126&itemno=R525L.

What is the HPV shot?

Human papillomavirus (HPV) is one of the most common STIs, with about 14 million people becoming infected each year, according to the Centers for Disease Control.[5] Some types of HPV are harmless and go away on their own, but others are very serious and can cause cervical, vaginal, or vulvar cancer. But the good news is that unlike with most STIs, there's a vaccine for HPV. That means you can get a shot from your doctor that can prevent you from getting some (but not all) strains of HPV, just like the shots you've probably gotten to prevent you from getting diseases like polio or chicken pox. It's most effective if you get it before you've had any sexual activity, but you can still get the vaccination even if you're already sexually active. Talk to your doctor, parent, or other trusted, knowledgeable adult to confirm you have been vaccinated or learn how to get vaccinated.

How do you use a condom?

A condom is a thin, flexible covering that goes over a penis during sex. If you use it right, it creates a barrier that semen can't get through, which reduces the risk of unwanted pregnancies and STIs. Condoms come in many different styles, sizes, and materials. There are even female condoms, which are placed inside the vagina instead of over the penis. Most condoms are made of latex, but for people who are allergic to latex, there are also polyurethane condoms.

The only problem is that if the condom rips, or if it's put on incorrectly and slips off, it's no longer effective at preventing STIs and unplanned pregnancies. See page 146 for a step-by-step guide on how to use a condom correctly.

How to Use a Condom

STEP 1   Get consent! For two people to have sex, they both have to say yes and continue to say yes the whole time. Consent is active, continuous, and never silent!

STEP 2   Check the expiration date on the back of the condom wrapper. You don't want to use an expired condom because it has a higher risk of breaking.

STEP 3   Open the condom wrapper carefully. Don't use your teeth, or you may accidentally tear the condom.

STEP 4   Make sure the rim of the condom is on the outside—otherwise you're putting it on inside out. Then pinch the tip of the condom to remove any air, place it on the head of the penis, and roll it down to the base of the penis. The penis has to be erect, or the condom won't stay on properly.

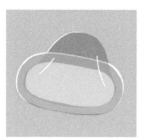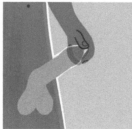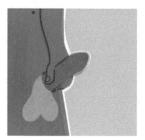

STEP 5 Have sex, and enjoy! You might want to use a water-based lubricant on the outside of the condom, which reduces the risk of the condom breaking and can also make sex feel better. Do not use an oil-based lube like baby oil or Vaseline; these can sometimes cause the condom to break.

STEP 6 After orgasm or ejaculation, hold the base of the condom in place and withdraw the penis from the vagina while it's still erect. (This keeps the condom from slipping off.) After the penis is out of the vagina, take the condom off, tie a knot in the end, wrap it in a tissue, and put it in the trash. Don't flush it down the toilet, because it might cause a clog.

Can I go to a doctor on my own?

It depends on what state you live in. However, at this point in your life, most doctors will ask your parents to leave the room at some point during a checkup. This is your opportunity to ask any questions you might feel embarrassed to ask in front of your parents. The doctor will not tell them what you say.

What is masturbation? How do girls masturbate?

Masturbation is when you rub or stimulate your genitals for pleasure, often to the point of orgasm, and it's totally normal and healthy. All people masturbate differently! For all our beginners, I suggest you start by using your clean hand to touch your clitoris, which is the most sensitive part of your vulva and has almost eight thousand nerve endings. That's a lot of power in a little place! There's no right or wrong way to do it: It's just a personal preference. Masturbation can be very important to figuring out what you like sexually. If you're uncomfortable masturbating, you're probably not ready to have sex yet.

Is it wrong to masturbate?

No! It's completely normal and healthy. I think masturbation is a great opportunity to learn about your body and what you like. How can you truly be ready for intercourse with another person if you don't know what you like? Also, masturbation is safe! There's no risk of STIs or unplanned pregnancy when you self-pleasure. Masturbation does not make you slutty, and it's not bad for your health. In fact, some studies show that it can relax you, help you sleep at night, and even reduce menstrual cramps.[6]

What does it mean when people talk about fingering a girl?

When people talk about fingering a girl, they mean touching her vulva and/or inserting fingers into her vagina. Fingering doesn't necessarily need to be done by another person—you can also do it yourself while masturbating. Wash your hands first so you don't bring bacteria into your vagina.

What is oral sex?

Oral sex is when one person uses their mouth to stimulate another person's genitals. Performing oral sex on a vagina is called "cunnilingus," while performing oral sex on a penis is called "fellatio." If you've heard people talk about "giving someone a blow job" or "sucking his dick," they were referring to fellatio.

Can I get an STI from oral sex?

Yes! It's possible to get an STI from giving or receiving oral sex. Having cuts in your mouth, like from flossing too hard, can make you more susceptible to getting an infection. Like with all sex acts, if you plan to have oral sex, you should use protection, like a condom or a dental dam (a thin sheet, usually made of latex). It's important that you and your partner have a conversation about getting tested and using protection before you engage in sexual activities.

Can I get pregnant from oral sex?

No, you can't get pregnant from oral sex. Your mouth is not connected to your reproductive system. Even if you swallow semen, the sperm could never get from your stomach to your fallopian tubes to fertilize an egg.

What is anal sex?

Anal sex is when the anus is penetrated instead of the vagina.

How do gay people have sex?

There is no "gay" way to have sex because the term "sex" does not hold the same meaning for all people. In addition, sexual activity is individual to each person or partner you encounter. Gay people can and do have sex in all the ways straight people do: kissing, touching, and vaginal, anal, and oral sex (sometimes with the help of sex toys or other special tools). There is always a risk associated with sexual acts that include the exchange of bodily fluids, like oral sex, anal sex, and vaginal sex. It is important that no matter how you identify—gay, straight, or somewhere in between—you speak with a trusted, knowledgeable adult and your partner about whether you are ready to become sexually active, what type of testing you should have before becoming sexually active, and what plan is in place if a "worst case" scenario happens.

Is girl-on-girl sex safer than boy-on-girl sex?

Girl-on-girl sex will not get you pregnant, but there is still a risk of STIs. It's important that you and your partner, whatever their gender, have a conversation about getting tested and using protection before you engage in sexual activities.

Is what I see in porn really how sex happens?

Pornography, or "porn" for short, is an image or video of people engaging in sexual activity. By now, you may have heard of it or even seen it on the Internet. The thing to remember about porn is that it's like any other form of entertainment we see on our screens. It's acting. Real sex doesn't look like what you see in porn, just like real life doesn't look like what you see in movies or on TV.

What is consent?

Consent is when you give permission for something to happen. When we're talking about sex, it's when both people actively say yes before engaging in physical contact. Consent is necessary before you have any sexual interaction with someone, and you have to give it out loud: You should never assume someone has consented to an activity if you haven't heard them say yes. You can take back your consent at any time—even if you've been making out with someone, or you've had sex with them before, or even if you're *currently* engaged in sex, that doesn't mean you can't say no to additional sexual contact. If someone keeps going and doesn't listen to you when you say no, that's sexual assault. Sexual assault is a crime, and you should immediately report it to the authorities or tell a trusted, knowledgeable adult.

How do I tell someone I don't want to have sex?

Sex between two people should only happen when both people want it. No one should ever pressure you into sex or make you feel like you have no choice (and you should never do that to anyone else). You never have to have sex with someone when you don't want to, even if you told them you would or if you've had sex with them before. If someone wants to have sex with you but you don't want to, don't be afraid to be very direct and to repeat yourself if you have to. You can say things like "I really like you, but I'm not ready for this right now" or "I'm not ready for sex, but I do like kissing you. Can we just keep doing that?" or "I just don't feel like it" or "No, you need to stop asking me." And don't hesitate to tell your trusted, knowledgeable adult if someone is trying to convince you to have sex when you don't want to.

What do I do if someone is trying to make me do things I don't feel good about doing?

No one has the right to force you to do things you don't feel good about. When someone pressures someone else to do something by using force or threats, it's called coercion. All people have the right to live free of sexual coercion and assault. If you have experienced someone forcing you to do something you're not comfortable with, it is not your fault, and you are not in the wrong. I understand it might be scary to tell someone what you're going through, but I urge you to not keep this to yourself. It's important to tell a parent or other trusted, knowledgeable adult so they can help you get out of this very difficult situation.

What is sexual abuse? What should I do if this is happening to me?

Sexual abuse is unwanted sexual behavior of any kind. Usually, when we talk about abuse, we're talking about an ongoing pattern, not a single event—one-time events are more often called sexual assaults. Sexual abuse can mean forced sexual intercourse, but can also be verbal abuse, someone showing you sexual images or sending you explicit text messages, someone exposing themselves to you, or any other unwanted sexual behavior. Any sexual behavior between an adult and a minor is always sexual abuse—a minor can't give consent for sexual activity with an adult. Sexual abuse is very serious, and if you are experiencing abuse yourself, you should immediately tell your trusted, knowledgeable adult or the authorities. This can be difficult, as abusers are often family members, teachers, or other people you may be close to or who seem to have a position of authority. But this behavior is never okay, no matter what, and you should never feel like you need to stay silent to protect someone else.

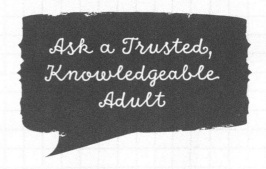

Ask a Trusted, Knowledgeable Adult

♥ Is it okay to masturbate?

♥ What should I do if someone asks me to do something I am not sure I'm cool with?

♥ If I get in a sticky situation and I need help, but I know I will probably get in trouble for it, will you still help me? How should I tell you about it?

Resources

Advocates for Youth

www.advocatesforyouth.org

Advocates for Youth partners with youth leaders, adult allies, and youth-serving organizations to advocate for policies and champion programs that recognize young peoples' rights to honest sexual health information; accessible, confidential, and affordable sexual health services; and the resources and opportunities necessary to create sexual health equity for all youth.

American Sexual Health Association

www.ashasexualhealth.org/sexual-health
/teens-and-young-adults

This association provides a wealth of resources on sexual health for both men and women, and specific resources directed at teens and young adults.

Amplify Your Voice

amplifyyourvoice.org/youthresource

Amplify is a project of Advocates for Youth, a national nonprofit that works to ensure the reproductive and sexual health and rights of young people.

Bedsider

bedsider.org

Providing accurate and honest information, this online birth control support network helps young women find the birth control method that's right for them and how to use it correctly.

Center for Young Women's Health and Young Men's Health

youngwomenshealth.org and
youngmenshealthsite.org

These websites provide information targeted at adolescents, including guides on a variety of sexual health topics such as contraception, STIs, LGBT health, and puberty.

Coalition for Positive Sexuality

www.positive.org

This website offers resources and tools for teens to take care of themselves and affirm their decisions about sex, sexuality, and reproductive control.

Coming Out Project (Part of the Human Rights Campaign)

www.hrc.org/explore/topic/coming_out.asp

The Coming Out Project helps LGBT and supportive straight people live openly and talk about their support for equality at home, at work, and in their communities each and every day. It offers FAQs about coming out, guides, and personal stories.

Equality Now

www.equalitynow.org

Lawyers Jessica Neuwirth, Navanethem "Navi" Pillay, and Feryal Gharahi founded Equality Now in 1992 with the mission of using the law to protect and promote the human rights of women and girls.

GirlsHealth.gov

girlshealth.gov/know-the-facts-first/index.html

Offering guidance to teenage girls, this website provides facts on sex and STIs, ways to protect yourself, and a testing center locator.

Go Ask Alice!

www.goaskalice.columbia.edu

Geared to young adults, this question-and-answer website contains a large database of questions about a variety of reproductive and sexual health concerns.

It's Your Sex Life

www.itsyoursexlife.com

Using an interactive website, MTV has resources for young adults on pregnancy, STIs and testing, LBGTQ, relationships, and consent, and a national hotline.

Love Matters

lovematters.in/en

This website offers a space to talk and ask questions openly and honestly about love, sex, and relationships for young adults around the world.

Love Is Respect

www.loveisrespect.org

Love Is Respect strives to be a safe, inclusive space for young people to access information and get help in an environment that is designed specifically for them. This website provides comprehensive education on healthy, unhealthy, and abusive dating relationships and behaviors.

Options for Sexual Health

www.optionsforsexualhealth.org

This online resource offers sexual and reproductive health care, information, and education from a feminist, pro-choice, sex-positive perspective.

The National Campaign to Prevent Unplanned Pregnancy

thenationalcampaign.org

The National Campaign to Prevent Teen and Unplanned Pregnancy is to improve the lives and future prospects of children and families and, in particular, to help ensure that children are born into stable, two-parent families who are committed to and ready for the demanding task of raising the next generation.

O.School

www.o.school

O.school is building a shame-free space by offering pleasure education through live streaming and moderated chat. At O.school, you can learn about sex and pleasure, join a diverse community, and share your own experiences.

Planned Parenthood Federation of America

www.plannedparenthood.org/teens

Providing up-to-date, clear, and medically accurate information, Planned Parenthood helps both young men and women better understand their sexual health.

RAINN

www.rainn.org

RAINN (Rape, Abuse & Incest National Network) is the nation's largest anti-sexual violence organization. RAINN created and operates the National Sexual Assault Hotline (800-656-HOPE, hotline.rainn.org) in partnership with more than 1,000 local sexual assault service providers across the country, and operates the DoD Safe Helpline for the Department of Defense.

Safe Teens

www.safeteens.org

Teenagers can use this youth-friendly website to find information on teen pregnancy, STIs, safe sex, relationships, and LGBTQ issues.

Scarleteen

www.scarleteen.com

This website provides a wealth of information for teens and young adults about sexuality, sex, and relationships, as well as advice and support, and even a safer sex shop.

Sex, Etc.

sexetc.org

Created for teens, by teens, this website provides accurate and honest information to improve teen sexual health, as well as various ways for adolescents to get involved in campaigns around sexual and reproductive health.

SexInfo Online

www.soc.ucsb.edu/sexinfo

SexInfo Online is a website devoted to comprehensive sex education based on the best research we have to date. Our primary goal is to ensure that people around the world have access to useful and accurate information about all aspects of human sexuality.

Stay Teen

stayteen.org

Using videos, games, quizzes, and a sex education resource center, this website delivers quality information about sex, relationships, abstinence, and birth control for teens.

Teen Health

teenshealth.org/teen/sexual_health

Adolescents can use this website to learn facts about sexual health, including articles about puberty, menstruation, infections, and birth control.

Youth Guardian Services

www.youth-guard.org

Youth Guardian Services supports the well-being of gay, lesbian, bisexual, transgendered, questioning, and straight supportive youth. At this time the organization operates solely on private donations from individuals.

Youth Resource

www.youthresource.com

In partnership with Advocates for Youth, this website is created by and for LGBTQ young people and provides information and support through education and advocacy.

End Notes

[1] http://www.advocatesforyouth.org/parents/136-parents

[2] Future of Sex Ed. "National Sexuality Education Standards." Accessed October 23, 2017. www.futureofsexed.org /documents/FoSE-Standards_WEB.pdf

[3] https://www.law.berkeley.edu/php-programs/courses /fileDL.php?fID=4051

[4] https://www.ncbi.nlm.nih.gov/pmc/articles/PMC3064497

[5] Centers for Disease Control. "Genital HPV Infection—Fact Sheet." Accessed October 31, 2017. www.cdc.gov/std/hpv /stdfact-hpv.htm

[6] https://www.plannedparenthood.org/learn /sex-and-relationships/masturbation

Topic Index

SELF-ESTEEM

SOCIAL MEDIA AND LIFE ONLINE

About the Author

MICHELLE HOPE is not your average sex-ed teacher! As an award-winning, passionate edu-tainer, she combines her love of pop culture, entertainment, and sexuality into opportunities that educate and motivate. With a master's degree in human development, as well as extensive post-graduate training in sexuality, Michelle is well-rounded in her ability to captivate and educate across various populations. With over 10 years of experience, she has delivered lectures across the country, and developed and implemented dynamic and creative sex-ed programming for youth and practitioners who serve youth communities.